Experiencing God in the Supernatural Newly Revised

Prophetic Acceleration

Jonathan Ferguson

Copyright © 2013 Jonathan Ferguson
All rights reserved.

ISBN: 1490980563
ISBN 13: 9781490980560

In this New Era of the Church embarking on its Kingdom mandate, it is essential that we learn to do whatever we do, as GOD's partner. Jonathan Ferguson's "Experiencing GOD in the Supernatural" is a GOD-given tool to help us reposition ourselves to represent heaven's realities here in the earth. This is a 'Must Read'.

Craig Ferguson
Sr. Financial Systems Analyst (FedEx)/Jonathan Ferguson's Father
2007 Dean of Wagner Leadership Institute/Memphis (Founded by Peter C. Wagner)
Founder of the Gateway Center

"Ferguson shares a wealth of knowledge which opens up our understanding of the realm of supernatural power of God and its flow and involvement in our lives. This book will bring clarity to the gifts of the Holy Spirit and increase your hunger for the things of God and for a deeper relationship with Him!"

---Bishop Dale C. Bronner, D. Min.
Founder/Senior Pastor/Author
Word of Faith Family Worship Cathedral

This book is powerful…explosive!

Damita Haddon
PDH Ministries/International Recording Artist/Psalmist

Contents

INTRODUCTION/IMPARTATION

CHAPTER 1

THE DEPTHS OF PRAYER & THE FULLNESS OF THE SPIRIT

-Understand the importance of living in the fullness of the Holy Ghost
-Learn how to distinguish between the evidence of having been filled with the Holy Ghost vs. the fruit of the Spirit
-Explore diversities of tongues: Distinguish speaking in tongues as a *gift of the Spirit* and speaking in tongues as a *prayer language*
-Understand why we should pray in unknown tongues and acknowledge multiple scriptural benefits of doing so
-Understand why praying in tongues is key in birthing the supernatural

CHAPTER 2

PROPHETIC DIMENSIONS OF THE SUPERNATURAL

-Understand the supernatural by defining the prophetic
-Discover three different dimensions of the supernatural mentioned in 1 Corinthians 12: 4-6 as follows: Gifts, Administrations, & Operations
-Explore the three different dimensions of 1 Corinthians 12 in context of the prophetic as follows: Gifts= the gift of prophecy, Administrations= the office of the prophet, Operations= the spirit of prophecy
-Explore the gift of prophecy and understand why the prophetic is a gift of the Spirit that should be desired
-Explore the office of the prophet and learn six Hebraic words that both define the office of the prophet and clarifies the job descriptions of the prophet
-Explore the spirit of prophecy and understand the correlation between Pentecost and the prophetic

Chapter 3

Spirit of Prophecy: Levels of Prophetic Revelation

-Understand more specifically what it actually means to experience God in the supernatural by defining what prophetic revelation is
-Continue to understand the spirit of prophecy
-Understand multiple levels of prophetic revelation
-Discern and embrace over 21 ways that God communicates and interacts with all believers as follows: Impressions, dreams, visions, levels & degrees of seeing in the Spirit, trances, outer body experiences, God's audible voice, angelic encounters, visitations of Jesus, and more
-Understand how to stir up, activate, and access revelation: Embracing God Encounters

Chapter 4

Prophetic Acceleration: The relevance of Revelation

-Embrace why it is important in the life of every believer to both understand and properly engage the supernatural
-Understand what prophetic acceleration is
-Understand the benefits of a God encounter
-Become opened minded concerning the things of the spirit
-Avoid heart conditions that lead to blasphemy
-Distinguish the divine from the demonic: Prophetic movements vs. occult movements
-Understand the difference between prophecy & divination
-Understand the difference between signs & wonders and false signs & wonders

Chapter 5

The Angelic Kingdom

-Gain a healthy perspective and appreciation for the angelic kingdom
-Broaden your concept of heaven and angelic structures within

heavenly places
-Understand the governmental structure of angles and their chain of command
-Understand different angels, how they look, and what they are assigned to do both in the heavens & in the earth
-Understand angelic activity & assistance in the life of the believer

Chapter 6

OPEN HEAVENS

-Understand what an open heaven is: Get an open heaven concept
-Study the realms of heaven (1st, 2nd, 3rd heavens)
-Learn how to know when the heavens are closed
-Understand what happens when the heavens are opened
-Understand how to open the heavens
-Understand heaven as a literal place
-Understand the relationship and correlation between the kingdom of God and open heavens

Introduction/Impartation

"And it shall come to pass in the last days, saith God, I will poor out of my Spirit upon all flesh…"
Acts 2:17

As a result of fasting, prayer, searching the scriptures, and a series of divine encounters, this book was compiled so that the reader could understand how much of God one could experience in this lifetime, why these experiences are important, and how they are available to everyone through Jesus Christ.

What does it mean to Experience God in the Supernatural?

Experiencing God in the Supernatural is about getting to know the Lord Jesus in a real way that extends beyond our initial faith in Him as a believer. In doing so, there is an invitation to work closely with Him on a consistent basis as sons and daughters in His Kingdom doing the works He has done and even greater (John 14:12). As believers, we should be interested in familiarizing ourselves with the supernatural aspects of authentic Christianity and doing the earthly work of the Lord's Kingdom until His return.

The scriptures teach that Eternal Life consists of "knowing God" (John 17:3). The word "know" here literally means to know intimately through experience. This book is a tool to help guide and coach us beyond the intellectual and rational aspects of relationship with HIM, into a measure of intimacy that is gained through ongoing experiences of HIS nature.

One of the Christian faith's greatest distinctions from other religious faiths is that the Lord actually "reveals" Himself through various encounters in order to make Himself known. In Christ Jesus, there is an invitation to transcend the natural ultimately for the purposes of experiencing and comprehending the fullness of God. These encounters are not merely an experience of phenomenon, but they are literally the way that close relationship with our heavenly Father is engaged, sustained, and enjoyed.

Why should you read this book?

A study on the supernatural is very broad; therefore, it is my goal to help individuals understand the supernatural from a scriptural perspective by defining the prophetic. In doing so, the reader will embrace the vast biblical extent of man's interactions with God, explore various dimensions of the Spirit realm, and learn what it means to live under and open heaven. In fact, this book will cover over 21 ways in which God may choose to interact or communicate with us as believers, plus more valuable information pertaining to the supernatural as is listed on the table of contents.

This is a book of both information and impartation. The pages of this book will literally come alive, as there have already been testimonies of various God encounters from those who have previously reviewed the writings contained. You will not only read this book, but you will experience what you read, and the things you learn will stir up the gifts that are on the inside of you. Get ready to take the limits off of your life. Get ready to be accelerated in the prophetic, because God is about to blow your natural mind with a supernatural revelation. I reiterate that this is not merely a book. This is an impartation.

Chapter 1

The Depths of Prayer & the Fullness of the Spirit

"...but be filled with the Spirit;" Ephesians 5:18

Key Points:
- Understand the importance of living in the fullness of the Holy Ghost
- Learn how to distinguish between the evidence of having been filled with the Holy Ghost vs. the fruit of the Spirit
- Explore diversities of tongues: Distinguish speaking in tongues as a *gift of the Spirit* and speaking in tongues as a *prayer language*
- Understand why we should pray in unknown tongues and acknowledge multiple scriptural benefits of doing so
- Understand why praying in tongues is key in birthing the supernatural

The infilling of the Spirit is an enduring and continuous experience in God. In fact, the Bible admonishes every believer to live a life full of the Spirit, yet without a Holy Ghost baptism we lack the capacity to do so. By the way, if you do not understand what a Holy Ghost baptism is, you will in just a moment. And not only will you embrace why the baptism important, but you will also understand why a strong prayer life is essential in living such a life in the fullness of the Holy Ghost.

You see, as we are filled with God's Spirit, one of the many benefits we receive is the ability to speak to God in a language that we have never been taught. This is called speaking in tongues or praying in tongues, which is a spiritual empowerment- another thing that we will understand in great detail throughout this chapter. And it is only as we use our God-given ability to pray in tongues that we will increase our capacity to break through barriers in prayer that attempt to hinder us from experiencing the fullness of God in our lives.

For this reason, I designed this chapter to explore some fundamentals of the Spirit filled life with you and also remove any confusion or misunderstanding that would hinder you from stepping into a fervent lifestyle of praying in tongues. It is only wise to lay such a solid foundation in prayer due to the extreme intensity of revelation truth contained within this book. As you take a moment within part one of this chapter to cover some basics with me, I can assure you that by the time you reach part two of this chapter, you will be glad that you have decided to take the journey.

We will begin our study by examining Holy Ghost baptism and also learning what both the evidence and the fruit of Holy Spirit infilling consist of. This information will serve as a foundation in understanding one of the many benefits of the Holy Ghost baptism, which is "speaking in tongues." Ultimately we will examine the subject of "speaking in tongues" and scripturally show the results that it brings to our prayer lives as it relates to the Supernatural.

Holy Spirit Baptism

If we are going to understand the fullness of the Spirit we must understand the baptism of the Spirit. And if we are to understand the depths of prayer we must understand the power of speaking in tongues, which in fact also comes in result of the baptism of the Spirit. However, speaking in tongues and being filled with the Holy Spirit have become subjects of great controversy. In fact, I believe the enemy hinders revelation in this area because he knows that the baptism of the Spirit is the gateway into the supernatural.

Some believe that individuals are filled with the Holy Spirit at salvation. Others believe that if a person has not spoken in tongues, he or she is not yet filled with the Holy Spirit. The problem with both opinions is that they both have faulty premises. The scriptural approach to speaking with tongues and being filled with the Holy Spirit is from a rather different perspective than that of our opinions and denominational doctrines, and we must become well versed concerning the subjects at hand.

To begin, we should understand that God desires His Spirit to be both "within" and "upon" us. And with that in mind we should next embrace the fact that there are multiple ways that the scriptures articulate those very realities. In fact, the terms and phrases that describe the Holy Spirit coming both within and upon the believer are as follows: receiving, being filled, and the baptism of the Holy Ghost.

Furthermore, it helps to know that the phrase "baptism in the Holy Ghost," is only directly quoted by John the Baptist and Jesus in the New Testament. After Pentecost, this same baptism of the Spirit is articulated as "being filled" or "receiving the Holy Ghost". Let me make it plain. Throughout the book of Acts whenever a person experienced the Spirit baptism, it was articulated as a person both "receiving" or "being filled" and in reference to the Holy Ghost both coming "within" and "upon" them! (See Acts 1:5-8; 2:4; 10:44-47; 11:16-17; 19:2-6).

For example, Holy "Spirit" and Holy "Ghost" both pertain to the same essence, which is the existence of the Spirit of God. Likewise, whether the scripture speaks of a person receiving the Holy "Ghost", or being filled with the "Spirit", the different phrases are still speaking of the same reality. We should not allow different usage of words or diversity concerning how this truth is articulated cause misunderstanding or confusion.

The difference between the fruit and the evidence of Holy Spirit Infilling

Now as it pertains to determining what the actual proof is that a person has received a Holy Spirit baptism is where things seem to get complicated, but in reality it's simple to discern. In the end, whether we agree or disagree concerning when a person is initially filled/baptized with the Holy Spirit, we cannot deny the results of one who is consistently being filled. And if we are not constantly being filled, we are most likely no longer hungering and thirsting after righteousness, or we were never really filled initially. The proof is in the pudding.

A believer should be able to recognize another spirit filled believer by the evidence and fruit that shows. We will better understand this truth as we understand the difference between the "fruit" of the Holy Spirit and the "evidence" of the Holy Spirit. And the two are very easy to distinguish.

Jonathan Ferguson

The fruit of the Holy Spirit is character yet the evidence is power. The evidence comes as a result of being filled with the Holy Ghost, yet the fruit comes by being led by the Holy Ghost. Just because we "have been" filled with the Holy Ghost does not mean that we "are being" led by the Holy Ghost even though we should (Galatians 5:25). We should be careful to embrace both the development of character (fruit) that comes through being led by the Spirit and the evidence of power that comes as result of being filled with the Spirit. Let's take a brief moment to further clarify before moving forward in this teaching.

I reiterate, the fruit of the Spirit is in reference to that which is cultivated in our lifestyle (Galatians 5:16-19). As we are "led by the Spirit", there is a work of the Holy Ghost at the core of our nature. However, the evidence of the Holy Ghost is yet in reference to the "signs" that accompany the Holy Ghost baptism.

Do you understand the difference yet? Let me explain it another way. The fruit of the Spirit is processed into our character and lifestyles over time. However, the sign that a person has initially received the Spirit of God is the power that is immediately evident their lives in one or many forms.

Jesus explained to us as believers that there will be a release of "power demonstrations" that follow us as "signs" in Mark 16:17-18. In fact, a "sign" can be defined as a demonstration of power. More specifically, speaking with "new tongues" is one of the power demonstrations mentioned in the previous context that Jesus promised would follow the believer in addition to casting out devils and healing the sick (Mark 16:17).

Jesus not only said that signs would follow us, but also made it very clear that this power for signs is not activated until after the Holy Ghost comes upon us[1] (See Mark 16:17-18; Acts 1:8; Luke 24:48-49). This is why speaking in tongues is considered as being the initial evidence of having received the Holy Ghost. If we have the Holy Ghost, we have power. If we have power, then we also have the tongues that come with the power.

When we are filled with the Holy Ghost we are empowered to speak with new tongues, cast out devils, heal the sick, and demonstrate the resurrection of Jesus. These signs have always been consistent in the lives of the believer who had received the baptism of the Holy Ghost throughout both New Testament and progressive church history.

It is also important we understand, concerning the power of the God, that casting out devils, healing the sick, and such like represent the empowerment of the Holy Ghost to serve God. Speaking in tongues however, is rather the empowerment through the Holy Ghost to commune with God. Furthermore, it is only as we are in proper communion with God that we can expect to see the maximum results in both serving God and the fruit of being led by Him.

Therefore, the ability to speak with new tongues is given to us by God so that our communion with Him through prayer is always secure and strengthened. When we speak in tongues in prayer we disconnect ourselves from relying on our personal capacity to connect with God. We no longer have rational limitations in our approach to prayer and we can expect God to do that which exceeds the abundance above all we can ask or think according to the power working inside of us (Ephesians 3:20).

Speaking in tongues is not something we do in order "to be" saved or filled with the Holy Spirit, but rather something we access because "we are" saved and filled with the Holy Spirit. Whether we agree or disagree concerning tongues being the evidence of being filled with the Spirit is least important. Despite any controversy we can never ignore the benefits available to the believer speaking with tongues, neither can we discredit that every believer can and should pray in tongues.

It will always come to the same conclusion no matter how technical we get. Are we filled with the Holy Ghost? Do we have integrity and character? Do we walk in love? Do we have power and do we speak with tongues? If we cannot answer yes to these questions we are lacking some key components in our Christian walk. Now that this foundation is laid, we will begin to deal with the subject of speaking with tongues and seek to encourage all believers to embrace the empowerment to speak in tongues along with its many benefits.

Jonathan Ferguson

Speaking in Tongues

Many people misunderstand the power of praying in tongues simply because of a lack of knowledge. I have also discovered that in our study of tongues it would help to first understand the difference between "the gift of the Holy Ghost" and "the gifts of the Spirit." The difference is that the Holy Ghost is a gift given from the Father, yet the "gifts of the Spirit" are gifts given by the Holy Ghost.

The "gift of the Holy Ghost" from the Father comes with an unknown tongue that empowers our prayer lives. However, there is yet a gift of the Spirit that is called "diversities of tongues", which is distinguished from the unknown tongue that empowers our prayer lives. As we study, we receive clarity regarding "speaking in tongues" activated in prayer as differing from the "tongues" that are activated when the gifts of the Spirit manifest (I Corinthians 12:7, 10).

The benefits of speaking in tongues in the context of prayer have nothing to do with the gifts of the spirit. When the New Testament believers were initially filled with the Holy Ghost, the spiritual gift "diversities of tongues" were not the tongues in manifestation as they were speaking in tongues in the upper room (Acts 2:1-4). We will understand this further as we obtain clarity on the subject of tongues by looking at the full biblical context.

The Ignorance Test Question: Do All Speak with Tongues?

> I Corinthians 12:1, 30
> (1) Now concerning spiritual gifts, brethren, I would not have you ignorant. (30) Have all the gifts of healing? do all speak with tongues? do all interpret?

As we clarify the context of this teaching, we can better answer the question from the previous text, "Do all speak with tongues?" We will only understand what Paul taught about "tongues" in I Corinthians 12:1, 30 as we understand in context of what Jesus taught about "tongues" in Mark 16:17. According to what Jesus taught in Mark 16:17, every believer can speak in tongues, yet what Paul teaches in I Corinthians 12:30 seems to contradict. Why is this? The answer is that there is more than one manifestation of what it means to speak in tongues. 5(1 Corinthians 12:10, 28; 1 Corinthians13:1). Therefore, the correct answer to 1 Corinthians 12:30, concerning whether all speak in tongues is dependent upon whether we understand what type of tongue this question is referring to. ⁱⁱ

In 1 Corinthians 12:30, the question concerning if all spoke in tongues only applies to a very specific type of tongues. And the answer is simple, as we understand that the way tongues manifest within the context of spiritual gifts will be different than the way tongues manifest within your prayer life. All believers can "speak in tongues" in the context of a prayer language, but all do not "speak in tongues" within the context of "diversities of tongues". The teaching within first Corinthians can become confusing when we over generalize both the context of speaking with tongues and the need for interpretation when speaking in tongues. Many have been hindered from a lifestyle of praying in tongues simply because they either believe that "speaking in tongues" is just not for them or just not that important. Others have been restricted because they have been told that they should not speak in tongues without an interpretation. The only way to prevent this tragedy is to be sure we understand the subject of speaking in tongues thoroughly.

Speaking in Tongues and Interpretation

As we briefly deal with speaking in tongues and interpretation, the information will yet require thorough reading and much meditation for many who may not be familiar with the verses that will be incorporated into the teaching. I recommend that the teaching be reviewed repeatedly so that key precepts are grasped and understood.

There is no scriptural law that a person cannot "pray in tongues" without an interpretation (1 Corinthians 14:39). In fact, the scriptures encourage us to strengthen and edify ourselves as much as possible by praying in tongues (Jude 20). We should be free to do this both in our private prayer lives and in the public gathering of believers.

The ONLY times that we are obligated not to speak in tongues without an interpretation is when the spiritual gift "diversities of tongues" are in operation. The reason being is that the gift "diversities of tongues," is a means by which a divine message can be delivered from God through one believer to another in order to edify the public gathering of believers. An interpretation would therefore be needed so that the message could be understood.

On the contrary, God has given us the empowerment to speak to Him in an unknown tongue as an alternative means of communication. This is called a prayer language or praying in the Holy Ghost. There is no need to interpret this tongue given to us as a prayer language even during the public gathering of believers. There is therefore a need to clarify by contextual evidence "what tongue" a particular scripture is referring to when "tongues" are mentioned in reference to interpretation so that we do not follow the error of teaching that believers should not speak to God in tongues in public church settings.

First Corinthians chapter fourteen shows great distinction between two different functions of speaking in tongues within the same chapter. At times Paul mentioned "speaking in tongues" in reference to a prayer language. At other times he mentions "speaking in tongues" in reference to the gift of the spirit called "diversities of tongues." The only way to distinguish the two is to allow scripture to interpret scripture.

For example, according to 1 Corinthians 14:12, 26, we know that one purpose for the gifts of the spirit is to edify the public gathering of believers. Therefore, in scripture whenever "speaking in tongues" is mentioned in a way to edify the public gathering of believers on a corporate level, it is in reference to the gift "diversities of tongues." On the contrary whenever speaking in tongues is mentioned in ways to edify the individual believer on a personal level, it is in reference to a prayer language.

Understanding the previous gives an explanation to why in 1 Corinthians 14:28 Paul commands not to speak in tongues without an interpretation yet in 1 Corinthians 14:39 he also commands that we DO NOT instruct believers to refrain from speaking in tongues in the public gatherings. It is because one "tongue", when interpreted, is a means to communicate revelation, knowledge, or teaching from one believer to another (1 Corinthians 14:6, 26-28). The other tongue is designed for us to edify ourselves and communicate directly to God (1 Corinthians 14:2, 4, 14, 28).

Many over emphasize the tongue that needs interpretation, while under-emphasizing the tongue that doesn't. Scriptures speak more concerning speaking in tongues as a prayer language in first Corinthians chapter fourteen than it does in reference to "diversities of tongues". In fact, the one and only time in first Corinthians fourteen that we are told not to speak in tongues without an interpretation, which is in reference to "diversities of tongues", is in 1 Corinthians 14:28, which by the way is often taken out of context by the reader and the teacher. Let's look at this scripture in proper context.

> 1 Corinthians 14:2, 27-28, 39
> (2) For he that speaketh in an unknown tongue speaketh not unto men, but unto God: for no man understandeth him; howbeit in the spirit he speaketh mysteries. (27) if any man speak in an unknown tongue….let one interpret (28) But if there be no interpreter, let him keep silence in the church; and let him speak to himself, and to God. (39) Wherefore, brethren, covet to prophesy, and forbid not to speak with tongues.

Many partially quote 1 Corinthians 14:28 in an unbiblical way teaching that believers should not speak in tongues in public without an interpretation, yet in order to understand the text we must take the whole verse and chapter into thought, study, and meditation. Verse two of the previous text along with verses four and fourteen explain the power of speaking in tongues when the tongue is directed towards God as a prayer language.

On the contrary, verses twenty-seven and twenty-eight are rather dealing with the gift diversities of tongues which is why the believer is told not to speak in tongues without an interpretation. However, verse twenty eight in proper context actually instructs the believer not to speak in tongues in a public setting without an interpretation UNLESS the believer is speaking in tongues in a way that is directed towards God or edifying himself. In fact, the scripture in verse thirty-nine furthermore instructs that speaking in tongues should not to be forbidden in public worship settings (1 Corinthians 14:39).

It is error not to teach 1 Corinthians 14:28 in its entirety. Truth is that the scripture does not merely say not to speak in tongues without an interpretation. And although it says to keep silence if there is no interpretation for the diversities of tongues, it also encourages the believer to rather speak to God in tongues. In fact, read I Corinthians 14:28 again in its entirety and compare it with I Corinthians 14:2. You will notice something very powerful in the text.

The revelation is that I Corinthians 14:28, which is the main scripture that many use to hinder individuals from speaking in tongues, actually reinforces the benefits of why I Corinthians 14:2 teaches that we should in fact pray in tongues. Now think about this for a moment. The scripture is saying that we will accomplish more praying in tongues than we will otherwise attempting to deliver a message to someone in an unknown language without an interpretation of that message. Be honest with yourself. Doesn't that make more sense than teaching people not to speak in tongues in public?

I want to warn you that as you continue to read your life will be changed forever. And once you begin to understand why speaking in tongues is so powerful, you will never believe the lies you have been told concerning why you should not speak in tongues. Buckle your seat belt because at this point there is no turning back. You are about to begin to experience God in the supernatural in ways you have never imagined.

Now that the foundation has been laid we must understand that there are many reasons why we should pray in tongues according to scripture. I believe the enemy fights against the believer's knowledge in this area because of the power that can be released. There are some things that will only be released as we pray more in the Spirit. Let's take the remainder of the chapter to understand the many benefits available to the believer who develops a discipline of praying in the Holy Ghost. In doing so we will discover why a lifestyle of praying in tongues unlocks a depth in prayer that is key pertaining to the believer's experience of God in various supernatural ways.

The Depths of Prayer Part Two

Benefits of Praying in Tongues:

1. We Speak Mysteries: We Receive Revelation

> 1 Corinthians 14:2
> For he that speaketh in an unknown tongue speaketh not unto men, but unto God: for no man understandeth him; howbeit in the spirit he speaketh mysteries.

The scriptures denote that when we speak in tongues we speak in a mystery. A mystery is simply the hidden wisdom of God (1 Corinthians 2:7-10). It would take more than an eternity to even begin to conceive all the knowledge of God, because His ways are past finding out. God understands that there are things that He wants to do that our lack of faith could possibly hinder. So in turn He gives us an unknown tongue to proclaim things that our minds don't have the capacity to understand in the natural (1 Corinthians 14:14), so that as we pray, the hidden wisdom and revelation of God can be released in the Spirit (1 Corinthians 2:7-10). As we pray, the mysteries of what God desires and plans to do are released in faith so that the manifestation has a landing strip or way to enter into the earth. As we proclaim the mysteries of God we are preparing the way in the Spirit for the next thing God wants to do and open up in our lives.

Mystery: can't be known vs. known by revelation

Another thing we should understand about a mystery is that it is not something that cannot be known. A mystery is rather something that can only be made known by way of revelation. When we pray in tongues we are praying things that can only be made known by revelation. This is important because where there is no revelation there can be no manifestation. As we pray in tongues, that which is a mystery to us in the natural is revealed to us in the Spirit. As we speak the mysteries of God in an unknown tongue, God opens up revelation to us and causes the things of the Spirit to become more real to us than things in the natural. And as this takes place the manifestation of what God wants to do in the earth can be accelerated.

Jonathan Ferguson

What is Revelation?

1 Corinthians 2:9-11
(9) But as it is written, Eye hath not seen, nor ear heard, neither have entered into the heart of man, the things which God hath prepared for them that love him. (10) <u>But God hath revealed them unto us by his Spirit</u>: for the Spirit searcheth all things, yea, the deep things of God. (11) For what man knoweth the things of a man, save the spirit of man which is in him? even so the things of God knoweth no man, but the Spirit of God.

The scripture referenced explains the power of revelation and it's process of unfolding in the believer's life. Revelation is the processor of all divine communication and experience, which we will cover in great detail in chapter three. There is great understanding given concerning revelation in 1 Corinthians 2:9-11, however, many stop reading at verse nine of scripture that says in short: "eyes have not seen, nor ears heard, neither has it entered into our hearts".

Many miss the revelation of 1 Corinthians 2:9-11 because they overlook 1 Corinthians 2:10, which is key to fully understanding the text in proper context. Verse ten, in short, says that God has "REVEALED THEM." And understanding the emphasis on "THEM" is key in understanding the spiritual truth in both verse nine and ten. The term "THEM," referenced in verse ten that God "REVEALS" by His Spirit is pertaining to the things that were covered from entering our eyes, ears, and hearts according to verse nine. Therefore, 1 Corinthians 2:9-11 is simply expounding upon the power of how things are revealed to us by the Holy Spirit.

The previous scripture is teaching us that the things prepared for us by God can be revealed to our eyes, to our ears, and in our hearts through the Spirit of God (1 Corinthians 2:9-11). In other words revelation is what activates our ability to see, hear, and experience divine things that normally go undetected by our natural senses. This is the type of revelation that is available as we pray in tongues. In fact, this is actually what happened in Acts 2:1-4, the first time the Holy Spirit empowered the prayer life of the believers in the upper room. Not only did they speak in tongues, but they began to "see" in the spirit tongues of fire, and they began to "hear" in the Spirit the sound of heaven, which was as a rushing wind.

2. We are Edified:

> I Corinthians 14:4
> He that speaketh in an unknown tongue <u>edifieth himself</u>; but he that prophesieth edifieth the church.

Edified: a built up strengthened spirit/inner man
(Ephesians 3:16-20)

Another thing that takes place as we pray in tongues according to the previous text is that we are edified. The word "edify" literally means to build up and strengthen. When we are praying in our own strength we have the tendency to "give in" before God "breaks in" and causes us to receive our "breakthrough". Therefore, our spiritual man must be strengthened in order to be conduits of God's regenerating power. At times our inner man becomes an incubator for what God wants to birth through our prayers. This is why our inner man must be strengthened and constantly built up.

For example, when Elijah wanted to birth the abundance of rain the scriptures indicate that he prayed seven times with his head between his knees, which was the birthing position of a Hebrew woman. It takes endurance and stamina to prevail in this kind of prayer. And at certain times praying in tongues is the only way we will acquire the maximum momentum required in pressing a prayer through the birthing canal of the Spirit. Therefore, when we don't know what to pray or when we feel too weary to pray is the perfect time to pray in the Holy Ghost. The revelation is that real power in prayer is activated as we first acknowledge our inability and inadequacy in prayer, only to next allow the Holy Ghost to pray through us (Romans 8:15, 26).

> I Corinthians 14:15
> What is it then? I will pray with the spirit, and I will pray with the understanding also: I will sing with the spirit, and I will sing with the understanding also.

In the previous text, when Paul speaks of praying in the understanding, he is speaking of praying in our native tongue. We should understand that prayer in the understanding can never exceed beyond our level of comprehension. Therefore, if there is no change after we have done all we know to do in prayer, it is only evident that we don't know all there is to know or be done in prayer. When praying in our native tongue, it's easier to pray below our maximum potential or to even pray amiss because we can only pray to the extent of our knowledge, which is limited. The problem with this is that our faith will never exceed our understanding. However, when we pray in the Holy Ghost not only do we edify ourselves but we build ourselves on our Holy faith...

> Jude 20
> But ye, beloved, building up yourselves on your most holy faith, praying in the Holy Ghost,

Jude 20 is telling us that we are built up as our holy faith is built up, which takes place as we are praying in the Holy Ghost. In other words, as we pray in the Holy Ghost, our Holy faith is built up and as our Holy faith is built up, we are built up. Understanding our Holy faith is the key in understanding the benefits of praying in the Holy Ghost.

The word Holy means separate, distinguished, and other than. Therefore, our Holy Faith is the faith that is distinct from our measure of faith (Romans 12:3). The measure of faith is the particular level of faith that any one of us walks in at any given moment. This means that our faith levels are different, but thank God that there is Holy Faith in the Holy Ghost. Our holy faith is a distinctive measure of faith that we access supernaturally by the Holy Ghost. The following scripture references show great examples of Holy faith.

Examples of Holy Faith:
Holy: separate, distinct from, other than

> Mark 2:5
> When Jesus <u>saw their faith</u>, he said unto the sick of the palsy, Son, thy sins be forgiven thee.

The previous scripture is a portion from the story concerning a man with the palsy that was forgiven and also healed by Jesus. The scriptures say that Jesus saw "their faith" which according to the context is not only in reference to the faith of the man with the palsy. The faith that Jesus saw had a lot to do with the faith of the friends that brought the man with the palsy to be healed according to Mark 2:3-4. Read it for yourself. You will see.

The faith of the man with the palsy was not the only faith in operation when he was healed. It was the faith of his friends, which was the faith that was "distinct" from his own faith in this case. This is very symbolic of Holy faith because it is representative of faith that comes from a source completely separate from our own measure of faith. The revelation is that when we in and of ourselves don't have the faith that God requires there is yet another faith that we can access by the Holy Ghost if we will pray in tongues. Now before you think that I have stretched my theology, lets look at the following text also as an example of Holy faith.

> Mark 9:24
> And straightway the father of the child cried out, and said with tears, Lord, I believe; help thou mine unbelief.

In Mark 9:24 notice the father's statement in the text, "I believe but help my unbelief." He was basically saying to Jesus that, "part of me is in doubt while part of me is accessing another source of faith." I believe that the father accessed the faith that was in Jesus Christ despite his tendency to his own doubt.

Our holy faith is the faith that the doubt of our minds cannot cancel out. Even when our minds start to doubt or waiver if we learn how to start praying in the Holy Ghost there is a faith that will build our spirits back up. This is the Holy faith in the Holy Ghost that we build as we pray in tongues. In fact, the word "building" in Jude 20 literally means to "super charge". This means that when we pray in the tongues not only do we build our faith, but also more specifically we literally super charge our Holy faith. There is power working inside of us that when activated can perform beyond our strongest belief and our utmost prayers (Ephesians 3:20).

> Ephesians 3:20
> Now unto him that is able to do exceeding abundantly above all that we ask or think, according to the power that worketh in us.

> Jude 20
> But ye, beloved, building up yourselves on your most holy faith, praying in the Holy Ghost,

Building up=supercharged

3. Our Spirits Pray:

> I Corinthians 14:14
> For if I pray in an unknown tongue, <u>my spirit prayeth</u>, but my understanding is unfruitful.

Another thing that takes place as we pray in tongues is that our spirits pray. This is significant in that our spirits are the core of who we are. If our spirits are praying, than it means that "the real us" is praying when we pray in tongues. In fact, not only do we pray out of our spirit man, but also because the Holy Ghost is infused within our spirit (I Corinthians 6:17), our spirits cannot pray without the Holy Ghost praying in agreement. Therefore in understanding the power of the Holy Ghost praying in and through us we will also understand the power of what our human spirits are impregnated with as we are praying in tongues. The following scripture will help us understand this truth.

> Romans 8:26-28
> (26) Likewise the Spirit also helpeth our infirmities: for we know not what we should pray for as we ought: but <u>the Spirit itself maketh intercession for us with groanings which cannot be uttered</u>. (27) And he that searcheth the hearts knoweth what is the mind of the Spirit, because he maketh <u>intercession for the saints according to the will of God</u>. (28) And we know that all things work together for good to them that love God, to them who are the called according to his purpose.

The previous scripture is talking about the power of how and when the Holy Ghost prays through us, but we must understand that it's not talking about speaking in tongues. We know that the scripture is not teaching of speaking in tongues because according to verse. 26 the prayer that the Holy Ghost prays through us is one that is without utterance. However, we must also understand that although the scripture is not teaching on speaking in tongues, the power of this scripture can still be activated as we speak in tongues. Again this is possible because our spirit will come into agreement with the Spirit of God when we pray in tongues. Although our spirits are praying when speaking in tongues, it is also scripturally considered "praying in the Holy Ghost" because of how the Holy Ghost is infused into and one our spirits (1 Corinthians 6:17).

We are called to "pray in the Holy Ghost" just as much as we are called to allow "the Holy Ghost to pray in and through us." "Praying in tongues" and the "Holy Ghost praying through us" are "two different functions" that activate the "same prayer power." It is clear in scripture that the Holy Ghost can pray through us a perfect intercession in groanings that we cannot put into words (Roman 8:27). It is also equally true that we can pray in the power of this perfect intercession as we pray in tongues. The difference is in understanding that when we pray in tongues, our spirits are leading the efforts in praying this perfect intercession (1 Corinthians 14:14). However, when the Holy Ghost prays through us He can at times take over in ways in which we cannot verbalize.

Above all else, according to Romans 8:26-28, praying in the Holy Ghost will cause us to walk in God's will. In fact, it is in the context of this Spirit empowered intercession that all things work together for our good (Romans 8:27-28). Holy Spirit empowered prayer always intervenes for us in ways that implement God's perfect will for our lives (Romans 8:27). Therefore, when dealing with the supernatural, praying in the Holy Ghost can prove to be of utmost importance because of how it can establish safe guards against spiritual error and fascination that attempts to draw believers out of God's will. A strong prayer life will keep our focus on Jesus the true and only source of that which is supernaturally pure.

The scriptures teach that as we seek the Lord in prayer, He will answer us and show us great and mighty things that we are yet to understand (Jeremiah 33:3). As we embrace a lifestyle of praying in tongues it will increase our capacity to comprehend and experience the different dimensions of God in the supernatural. Praying in tongues will strengthen our spirits and add endurance to our prayer lives. It will give us the stamina we need to increase our breakthrough capacity in prayer while most of all always centering us in the perfect will of God.

Jonathan Ferguson

This foundation of prayer will be essential as we continue to explore the supernatural. It will be impossible to comprehend the depths of the Spirit without stability and consistency in the area of prayer. The practice of prayer is the only legal way to connect our "natural" to the "super". We will discover that it is the discipline of prayer that protects and hides us from indulging the fascinations and error that lures many into a counterfeit supernatural.

Chapter 2

Prophetic Dimensions of the Supernatural

"May be able to comprehend with all saints what is the breadth, and length, and depth, and height; And to know the love of Christ which passeth knowledge, that ye might be filled with all the fullness of God." Ephesians 3:18-19

Key Points:
- Understand the supernatural by defining the prophetic
- Discover three different dimensions of the supernatural mentioned in 1 Corinthians 12:4-6 as follows: Gifts, Administrations, & Operations
- Explore the three different dimensions of 1 Corinthians in context of the prophetic as follows: Gifts= the gift of prophecy, Administrations= the office of the prophet, Operations= the spirit of prophecy
- Explore the gift of prophecy and understand why the prophetic gift of the Spirit that should be desired
- Explore office of the prophet and learn six Hebraic words that both define the office of the prophet and clarifies the job descriptions of the prophet
- Explore the spirit of prophecy and understand the correlation between Pentecost and the prophetic

Defining the Prophetic is Defining the Supernatural

Many use the term "prophetic" loosely and freely without having a full understanding or insight into the actual meaning. For many the prophetic has become another cliché word that only sounds good within our spiritual jargon. Truth is that it is impossible to be prophetic without understanding the heart and mind of God revealed in the scriptures of the bible. Likewise it is impossible to walk out the prophetic apart from the supernatural.

The Prophetic is very essential in dealing with the supernatural because it originates within an authentic experience with God Himself. Apart from man's ability to directly interact with God the prophetic would not exist. Therefore, understanding the prophetic and its many different dimensions of revelatory experience is key in understanding the Supernatural. Some understand the supernatural pertaining to levels of power, but many are yet to understand the supernatural pertaining to the realms of revelatory experience.

Supernatural Dimensions:

Before we begin to explore various dimensions of prophetic I believe we should first at least have a basic comprehension of what spirituals dimensions represent. A great place to start is a popular quote of Jesus in John 14:2 concerning the mansions in heaven.

John 14:2
In my Father's house are many mansions...

Although Jesus was talking about literal dwelling places in heaven, it is also interesting to note that Jesus used the concept of houses and mansions to explain a spiritual realm in heaven. Understanding spiritual dimensions is much like understanding a house or mansion that has many rooms. Dimensions distinguish the magnitude or the complete scope of a particular element. They bring definition to the height, the depth, the measure, and the extension of a specific domain or realm (Ephesians 3:18).

Simply put, a dimension is a measure of the whole scope. For example, a single slice of pie is a dimension of the whole pie. Dimensions, figuratively speaking, can be looked at as connecting the dots or putting pieces of a puzzle together.

The supernatural is a realm in the Spirit with multiple dimensions in which many experience through the prophetic. In other words, there are multiple dimensions of the supernatural that correlate directly with the prophetic. Therefore, prior to our examination of prophetic dimensions, a firm foundation of understanding can be laid by simply studying the teachings concerning the supernatural found in first Corinthians chapter twelve. As we examine Paul's teaching on the supernatural it will help us begin to embrace the vast dimensions of the supernatural as it correlates to the prophetic.

Paul Teaching the Supernatural

> I Corinthians 12:1
> Now concerning spiritual *gifts*, brethren, I would not have you ignorant.

Paul is teaching so that we are not ignorant about the Supernatural (I Cor 12:1 "spirituals") not just the spiritual gifts.

Although the gifts of the Spirit are mentioned in the teachings of I Corinthians 12, the gifts of the Spirit are not the primary focus of the context. In fact the word "gifts" in I Corinthians 12:1 is italicized meaning it was not there in the original text. Although the word "gifts" is mentioned in chapter twelve it is not mentioned in verse one of chapter twelve. Therefore, the correct way to read verse one of chapter twelve is "Now concerning the spirituals, brethren, I would not have you ignorant."

The word "spirituals" in the text is speaking of the supernatural. Paul was literally saying that he didn't want us to be ignorant concerning the supernatural. Paul was teaching more holistically concerning the realm of the Spirit in which he also expounded on the spiritual gifts as well as other spiritual truths. When we lessen the weight of first Corinthians chapter twelve to merely spiritual gifts teaching, we automatically limit ourselves to about a thirty percent comprehension level of what the text is introducing to the believer.

> **I Corinthians 12:4-7**
> (4) Now there are <u>diversities of gifts</u>, but the same Spirit. (5) And there are <u>differences of administrations</u>, but the same Lord. (6) And there are <u>diversities of operations</u>, but it is the same God which worketh all in all. (7) But the manifestation of the Spirit is given to every man to profit withal.

According to the previous reference, it is clear that as we delve further into first Corinthians chapter twelve, we will understand three distinct dimensions of the Supernatural and not just Spiritual Gifts. In I Corinthians 12:4-6, three dimensions of the supernatural are introduced to the believer. The three dimensions of the supernatural that

Paul introduces include gifts, administrations, and operations. There are different levels, measures, and degrees of walking in the supernatural. Therefore we cannot be narrow minded in comprehending revelation and manifestations of the Spirit of God (Ephesians 3:18).

Three Distinct Dimensions:

Gifts= inspiration; charisma; divine influence

Administrations = service; office

Operations = energy; activity; movement

Prophetic Dimensions:

The prophetic is "one" of the multiple manifestations of the spirit that exists within all three dimensions of the supernatural covered in the teachings of Corinthians. There is a prophetic gift, a prophetic administration, and a prophetic operation of the supernatural. The gift of prophecy is the prophetic gift, the office of the prophet is the prophetic administration, and the spirit of prophecy is the prophetic operation. Although there are many other prophetic functions, exploring these three dimensions of the prophetic will serve as a foundation in understanding the supernatural. For the remainder of the chapter we will take time to explore the three dimensions of the prophetic that directly correlate with the three dimensions of the supernatural mentioned in 1 Corinthians 12:4-6.

Gifts = gift of Prophecy

Administration = office of the Prophet

Operations = spirit of Prophecy

Intro to Gift of Prophecy: Lacking No Gift

The first dimension of the prophetic to explore is the gift of prophecy, but just before we do so lets embrace a key truth in understanding the gifts of the Spirit and how they are available to every believer. We should begin in understanding that there is a capacity in every believer for the Holy Spirit to manifest all nine gifts of the Spirit throughout our various walks with Christ. The previous statement seems hard for us to accept only until after we begin to understand that the Spiritual gifts are the lowest dimension of walking in the Supernatural just as much as personal prophecy is the lowest dimension of the prophetic. In fact, the Corinthian church had all nine gifts of the Spirit in operation and Paul said of them that they were still yet carnal (I Corithians 3:3).

Maturity only comes in the supernatural as one begins to embrace accountability and character. The highest place in the Supernatural is walking in an "oneness" relationship with the Lord (John 17:21-24). It is the fullness of God manifested in our bodies (Ephesians 3:19). It is Jesus inside of us, the hope of glory (Colossians 1:27). The highest realm in the supernatural is to know Jesus and be conformed into His very image (Romans 8:29). Therefore, the ability to function in all nine gifts of the Spirit should not be something beyond our comprehension or spiritual capacity as believers.

I Corinthians 1:7
So that ye come behind in no gift; waiting for the coming of our Lord Jesus Christ:

In order to live a lifestyle in which we come behind in no gift, we must first embrace the fact that a life that is lived in the Spirit consists of more than merely manifesting a few gifts of the Spirit ever so often. In addition to that, we should know that if there were a limitation on how many gifts that could manifest in a person's life, the scriptures would have never taught us to desire other gifts (I Corinthians 12:31). There must be a balance in understanding how God distributes the gifts to each of us and the desiring of other gifts (I Corinthians 12:11, 31).

All nine gifts of the Spirit are available and accessible to all believers. God wants us to be at the place where we position ourselves to allow any particular gift to flow through us whenever His Spirit desires. We can settle for how we are familiar with operating or we can press in for more. And if we are going to press in for more, the gift of prophecy would be a great place for starters, which is one of the reasons that we are taught to desire to prophesy (I Corinthians 14:1).

Desiring the Prophetic Gift

As we begin to explore the prophetic, one of the first things we learn is that there is a dimension in the prophetic called the gift of prophecy which can unlock what the scriptures speak of as a "more excellent way" of flowing in spiritual gifts (1 Corinthians 12:31-14:1). This is why as we explore the gift of prophecy we must first understand foundationally that all nine gifts of the Spirit are available to all believers. It's time that we not only know our prominent areas of gifting, but also the keys to flowing in and activating all nine gifts of the Spirit. We must embrace the fact that beyond receiving the gifts, we have received the Holy Spirit who manifests all of the gifts.

The More Excellent Way:

> 1 Corinthians 12:31
> But covet earnestly <u>the best gifts</u>: and yet shew I unto you <u>a more excellent way</u>.

> 1 Corinthians 14:1
> <u>Follow after</u> charity <u>(love)</u>, and <u>desire spiritual</u> *gifts*, <u>but rather</u> that ye <u>prophesy</u>.

The first thing we should give attention to, according to 1 Corinthians 12:31, is that there are some gifts of the Spirit that are preferred over others. Secondly, we should understand that there is a "more excellent way" of pursuing various gifts to be in operation in our lives. Lastly, according to 1 Corinthians 14:1, we should understand that the "more excellent way" of operating in the gifts is mentioned in the context of "love" and "the gift of prophecy," which are two key components that can act as a catalyst to ignite and release various gifts of the Spirit. In fact, the gift of prophecy has a history of pioneering the activation of multiple spiritual gifts. This truth is exemplified in the prophets of old, the life of Jesus, and in the early church.

However, the scriptural references concerning this level of prophetic activity, is rather frequently designated to those who walked in the fivefold offices of the Apostle, Evangelist, and Prophet. What I mean by this is that those who through the prophetic unction flowed in all nine gifts of the Spirit were people who were wholly given to the

Lord's official service in the ministry. Nevertheless, in Ephesians 4:11, a mandate is conveyed to equip the entire body of Christ. Therefore, scripturally the ability to walk in all nine gifts of the Spirit, I believe is not limited to the fivefold ministry. Although many have not arrived I believe it should still be our pursuit to press toward the mark.

If you have made it this far in your reading you are more than ready to go deeper in your understanding. However, before moving any further in the teaching we should understand what I refer to as "gift clusters" as a foundation in observing how the gift of prophecy acts as a catalyst to ignite other gifting manifestations.

Distinguishing the Gifts:

The gifts of the Spirit are often activated within clusters. A gift cluster is when one gift of the Spirit pioneers the activation of another gift of the Spirit, or simply when multiple gifts of the Spirit manifest simultaneously. It is often because of this that many cannot distinguish one gift of the Spirit from another especially if they are similar in manifestation. Therefore, it is important that the gifts of the Spirit are properly distinguished, which is simple to accomplish. The gifts of the Spirit can be classified within three divisions. There are also three spiritual gifts within each division as are listed as follows.

3 Gifting Classifications:

<u>Speaking gifts</u> = diversities of tongues, interpretation of tongues, gift of prophecy

<u>Power gifts</u> = gift of faith, gifts of healing, working of miracles

<u>Revelatory gifts</u> = word of knowledge, word of wisdom, discerning of spirits

There are many examples of gift clusters, yet more specifically whenever the gift of prophecy manifests, it is usually clustered along with a revelatory gift of the Spirit as well. This is why many confuse the gift of prophecy with the revelatory gifts of the Spirit, which are the word of knowledge, word of wisdom, and the discerning of spirits. The basic function for the gift of prophecy does not include within itself the divine knowledge, wisdom, or discernment contained within the revelatory gifts of the Spirit (1 Corinthians 14:3).

However, throughout scriptural examples, especially in the Old Testament, the revelatory gifts are categorized as prophecy because the prophetic word was the vehicle or conduit for them to be expressed. It is only as the gift of prophecy clusters with the revelatory gifts of the Spirit that the secrets of men's hearts are made known (1 Corinthians 14:24). Historically, not only did the revelatory gifts flow through prophecy in scripture, but also we clearly see elements of other spiritual gifts activated through the prophetic word. There are examples of what we can call prophetic gift clusters below along with definitions of the revelatory gifts.

Prophetic Gift Clusters:
(Other Gifts Activated in the Prophetic)

1. Word of Knowledge: (2 Kings 5:20-26)
Note: the divine knowing of a particular fact as opposed to acquired knowledge

2. Word of Wisdom: (2 Kings 3:15-20)
Note: the divine revelation or instruction into the future plans and/or purposes of God

3. Discerning of Spirits: (2 Kings 6:16-18)
Note: the word discern means to see; it is the ability to see into the unseen; this gift can reveal spirits, intentions, and motives

4. Working of Miracles: (1 Kings 17:11-16)

5. Gifts of Healing: (2 Kings 5:14-15)

6. Tongues and interpretation coupled together is equivalent to prophecy bringing comfort, edification, and exhortation. Therefore, when the gift of prophecy is in activation there is no need for diversities of tongues and interpretation to be in activation simultaneously.

7. Gift of Faith: Whenever prophecy is activated Faith is as well. (Romans 12:6)

In conclusion to exploring this particular dimension of the supernatural we should remember that prophecy is a gift that simply builds up (edification), stirs up (exhortation), and strengthens (comfort), according to 1 Corinthians 14:3. However, although it is simple, prophecy is powerful and explosive in that it can be the vehicle for other gifts to be activated and stirred through the spoken word as has been exemplified in the previous examples of prophetic gift clusters. This is one reason why we are "…rather to prophesy."

More on Dimensions of the Prophetic:

Let us take a minute to review our purpose of studying the dimensions of the prophetic. There are many realms and dimensions of the supernatural. There are also dimensions of the prophetic clearly mentioned in scripture other than the gift of prophecy. Being that Paul did not expound upon the three dimensions of the supernatural mentioned in first Corinthians chapter twelve completely, the prophetic can help us in our understanding because it is a manifestation of the Spirit existing within all three dimensions of the supernatural mentioned in 1 Corinthians 12:4-6.

We can cross reference the prophetic in order to gain more understanding of the supernatural. So far, through studying the gift of prophecy we have learned that all can access a dimension in the supernatural of flowing fluently in spiritual gifts. Because of this, it is easy to understand why the gifts of the Spirit are important pertaining to the supernatural. They literally become the means by which we become the vessels for others to experience the one true supernatural God just as we have. With that in mind, the next dimension of the prophetic to explore is the office of the prophet.

Exploring the Office of the Prophet

Prophetic Administration

Before engaging in a deeper study of the prophetic it is wise to distinguish the authority of one who walks in the prophetic office. The office of the prophet is the prophetic administration. And more particularly, the administrations of the supernatural are essential because they bring order. This is important to understand because many in our day and time operate in confusion in the name of spirituality.

It is important that we understand and embrace accountability to proper authority as we grow and mature in the things of the Spirit. We must learn that true spirituality never abandons the principles of submission and humility. On the contrary, the prophetic office is often self-appointed by those who begin to experience revelatory realms, but have not embraced proper protocol. For this purpose it is important to distinguish the prophetic grace (operation) and the prophetic office (administration).

> 1 Kings 19:16
> And Jehu the son of Nimshi shalt thou anoint to be king over Israel: and Elisha the son of Shaphat of Abelmeholah shalt thou anoint to be prophet in thy room.

The story of Elisha succeeding Elijah, which began in the previous text, is a great example of how prophetic ability does not validate prophetic office. In other words being prophetic does not make a person a prophet. There are many who may experience prophetic revelation, but it is the mantle of a prophet that distinguishes a prophet.

When we look at the context of this story in the book of kings concerning Elijah and Elisha, we understand that the office of the prophet is that which is sanctioned by God. Many were in Elijah's school of the prophets, but mere prophetic ability and gifting did not qualify them to take Elijah's placement of authority. Although there were many others with prophetic gifting, only Elisha was chosen to take the office of the prophet when Elijah was taken away. The mantel that was handed down to Elisha caused him to access a prophetic empowerment that transcended prophetic ability and gifting. It is necessary that we understand the prophetic mantle and be able to distinguish between prophetic gifting and prophetic office.

Six Hebraic Words Descriptive of the Prophet's Mantle

1. Nebuwah: those that foretell or predict

2. <u>Nabi</u>: the inspired man; the "official" prophet; to bubble up or stir up

The prophetic is an official administration within God's Kingdom. It is the "Nabi" function of the prophetic that distinguishes the prophet to serve as an ambassador with the full backing of Heaven's government. In fact, in Israel's ancient culture the prophet would be equivalent to someone that had a high-ranking military position, or someone who was a governmental official. Furthermore, Nabi not only speaks of the office of the prophet, but also the inspiration of the prophet. The inspiration aspect of Nabi is the means by which a prophet is continually sensitive to discern the activities of the Spirit realm from which he serves and has citizenship, which is undoubtedly heaven. In fact, the fire in Jeremiah's bones was the stirring and bubbling of prophetic inspiration. [1]

It is a consistent stirring and awakening of the gifts inside that brings about a prophetic awareness and corresponding action in the lives of God's prophets. God sanctions such ones as officers who exercise spiritual authority in cities, regions, and nations in favor of Heaven's will (Jeremiah 1:5, 10). Therefore, both the inspiration and the office aspects of Nabi are intertwined. They cause the prophet to first discern the activity of heaven and next have the authority and power to initiate the alignment of the activities in earth with those of heaven- all through a spoken word.

3. <u>Nataph:</u> to open the heavens; to ooze; distill; to fall in drops

The "Nataph" function of the official prophet is significant in that it is one of the elements that supernaturally causes the word of the Lord to be set in motion. A prophet is one who uses words to open the heavens. Communities, cities, and even nations can be changed as they speak because of how atmospheres, climates, and environments must adjust to their words. The spirit and words of a prophet has the power to produce a prophetic presence.

According to Deuteronomy 32:2, the words of Moses would "fall in drops" on the people like dew and rain as he spoke the word of the Lord. This is symbolic of Moses speaking under a prophetic anointing.

The intensity of his words pierced the atmosphere for open heaven manifestations.

In other words, the word of a prophet creates an atmosphere for what they say to come to pass. The same thing that occurred with Moses took place with Peter in Acts 10:44. Peter was preaching under a prophetic anointing when "while he was yet preaching" the Holy Ghost fell upon everyone that heard the word. The same is true throughout the ministry of Jesus, in that as He taught, power was present to heal the sick (Luke 5:17). Whenever Jesus taught the word, the atmosphere became conducive for miracles, signs, and wonders.

Another definition for the word "nataph" as we have seen is to distill, which has to do with cleansing and purification. There is a cleansing that comes in the prophetic utterance. This is why strong conviction and liberation often accompanies prophetic preaching.

> John 15:3
> Now ye are clean through the word which I have spoken unto you.
>
> Ephesians 5:26
> That he might sanctify and cleanse it with the washing of water by the word.

4. <u>Chozeh:</u> seer; those that see; the ability to receive a message through visual communication

> Habakkuk 2:1
> I will stand upon my watch, and set me upon the tower, and will watch to see what he will say unto me, and what I shall answer when I am reproved.
>
> Ezekiel 13:3
> Thus saith the Lord GOD; Woe unto the foolish prophets, that follow their own spirit, and have seen nothing!

Chozeh is the ability to see things in the Spirit and interpret the visions and images into a message. Prophets bring understanding, relevance, and can both accurately and plainly articulate spiritual things. This implies that the ability to see alone does not qualify the prophetic function of a "seer". Chozeh has a lot to do with the process of perception and interpretation concerning what is being seen.

This ability is one that is developed over time, as a prophet is equipped in all the aspects of "seeing". He or she then becomes competent in processing what is seen for prophetic delivery. Therefore, we can't completely examine "Chozeh" without examining other aspects of what it means to see in the Spirit. And there are many aspects of the seers anointing, but I only want to cover the "Roeh" and "Shamar" aspects of what it means to be able to see in the Spirit in reference to the office of the prophet.

5. Roeh: to see

> Psalm 23:1
> The LORD is my shepherd; I shall not want.

The word shepherd is descriptive of the pastoral anointing and derives from the original word "Roeh" which literally means, "to see". This aspect of spiritual vision deals with the release of progressive revelation, which causes prophets to know the divine counsels and instructions of God. It can also cause prophets to be born with a high inclination to creativity, which eventually causes them to become builders and trendsetters.

For this reason, the ability to see in the prophetic and the pastoral anointing go hand in hand. Could it be that David and Moses experienced aspects of their prophetic preparation while tending to sheep? It would make perfect sense being that the shepherd's job is to be able to look ahead and steer the sheep in the proper direction.

Prophets are needed to work very closely with pastors; at times, they also have the ability to pastor. They are well equipped to teach, impart, and train. This empowerment of spiritual vision enables prophets to disciple others because they not only master what they do, but they have the ability to train others to do the same. As they are looking ahead to see what direction the church should be going in, they are not only preparing people to move ahead, but they are also training others to maintain where the church has been. As this takes place, responsibilities are delegated normally through a type of ordination so that the church does not lose any ground gained as it moves on into its next dimension of effectiveness.

The prophet has a Shepherd's function of guidance and counseling to direct believers in the ways of the Lord. The history of the prophets show that the Roeh function was often used to offer counsel to the kings of Israel as "Seers", which is symbolic of the apostolic and prophetic collaborate. Prophets have great wisdom and apostolic insight that equips them as Divine strategist in the Kingdom of God. Competent prophets have apostolic grace and are even at times chosen by the Lord for apostolic succession and ordination. This is why most of the prominent prophets of the Old Testament had ministries that closely resembled the apostolic ministry patterned in the New Testament. In Fact, without apostolic and prophetic foundation, the pastoral anointing would have no basis of effectiveness (Ephesians 2:20).

6. Shamar: those that watch

Watching is inclusive of intercession and involves the ability to see danger from afar, sound an alarm, and stand guard. A strong prophet is a strong warrior and a strong intercessor (1 Kings 19:17). As warriors and intercessors they have the ability to both initiate things and stop things in the earth through prayer (Ezekiel 13: 4-5). Prophets are inclined to battle and their "shamar" function causes them to act as guardians and protectors. There are also angelic guards assigned to this prophetic function. Elijah and Elisha are great examples of prophets working in coalition with the Lord's army of Angels.

Examples:

2 Kings 2:12
And Elisha saw it, and he cried, My father, my father, the chariot of Israel, and the horsemen thereof. And he saw him no more: and he took hold of his own clothes, and rent them in two pieces.

2 Kings 6:16-17
(16) And he answered, Fear not: for they that be with us are more than they that be with them. (17) And Elisha prayed, and said, LORD, I pray thee, open his eyes, that he may see. And the LORD opened the eyes of the young man; and he saw: and, behold, the mountain was full of horses and chariots of fire round about Elisha.

2 Kings 13:14
Now Elisha was fallen sick of his sickness whereof he died. And Joash the king of Israel came down unto him, and wept over his face, and said, O my father, my father, the chariot of Israel, and the horsemen thereof.

The previous scriptures are important because they are in reference to the angels that accompanied the prophetic mantles of Elijah and Elisha. Shamar equips the prophet both offensively and defensively in spiritual war. Defensively, it can empower the prophet to expose and overthrow demonic war strategies (2 Kings 6:8-12). Offensively, it can empower the prophet to successfully pursue and conquer new spiritual territory while engaging in spiritual warfare.

Two other great examples of this is the angelic guard that accompanied the prophetic mantles of both Joshua and Isaiah. In Joshua 5:13 the angelic host helped Israel invade the city of Jericho. In Isaiah 37:21, 36 the angel of the Lord was released by the prophetic word of Isaiah to smite the Assyrian army. In fact, from the time that Joshua led the Israelites into the promise land the angelic hosts never ceased to accompany the succeeding prophetic mantles of Samuel, Elijah, and the like.

New Testament Descriptive for the Prophet:

A. The office of the prophet lays a solid foundation in the word of God concerning the believer's faith (Ephesians 2:20; Ephesians 3:1-6)
B. The office of the prophet has an administration of governments to establish and to order. (Ephesians 4:11; I Corinthians 12:28)

> The prophet has a platform of influence in leadership for instruction in spiritual maturity and growth.
> C. The office of the prophet imparts, confirms, and releases gifts and ministries
> (Acts 13:1-4; Acts 15:32)
> *Note: Apostles confirmed by prophets in Acts chapter thirteen gives credence that the apostolic and prophetic go hand in hand. The prophetic office also functions in a measure of mastery that can instruct and impart in the prophetic grace.
> D. The office of the prophet serves to bring important transitional messages to the body of Christ (Acts 11:26-30; Acts 21:10-14)

There are other things that can be learned concerning the prophetic mantle and office, but the objective of this book is to only cover the prophetic in context of the supernatural. One of the reasons for studying the prophetic administration is to understand the accountability that comes with our spirituality. Without righteous order and government the prophetic is nothing different than witchcraft and divination. The supernatural means nothing if there are no standards of holiness, accountability, character, and submission. The next dimension of the prophetic to be examined is the prophetic operation, which is the Spirit of prophecy.

Prophetic Dimensions Part Two

The Spirit of Prophecy: Exploring Prophetic Operations

We understand now to a certain extent the gift of prophecy, which is a gift of the Spirit. We have also learned about the prophetic office, which is an administration of the Spirit, but the spirit of prophecy is a completely different dimension of the supernatural. The Spirit of prophecy is classified among the "operations" of the Spirit (1 Corinthians 12:3-6). In other words the spirit of prophecy is the core of how the prophetic operates. It is a dimension consisting of many levels of revelatory experience.

In order to better understand the Spirit of prophecy we must understand the background of the book of Revelations. Therein, John is given what is known as the revelation of the Lord Jesus Christ in a series of various prophetic experiences. In Revelations 19:10, John comes into a greater understanding of what's taking place, as it is said to him that, "the testimony of Jesus is the Spirit of Prophecy." It is through the Spirit of Prophecy that we experience revelation that causes us to be aware of, respond to, or cooperate with what God is doing in our lives and how He is revealing Himself.

For this reason, the Spirit of prophecy is the testimony of Jesus. It is the broadest dimension in the prophetic in which we will cover different levels of revelation that will bring clarity in understanding the supernatural. We will also more embrace how God speaks and interacts with His people today. Now let's lay a firm foundation in understanding the basic functions of the Spirit of Prophecy.

Revelations 19:10
> And I fell at his feet to worship him. And he said unto me, See thou do it not: I am thy fellowservant, and of thy brethren that have the testimony of Jesus: worship God: for <u>the testimony of Jesus is the spirit of prophecy</u>.

What is the testimony of Jesus?

Testimony = God will do it again.
Hebrews 13:8
Jesus Christ the same yesterday, and today, and forever.

First and foremost, the testimony of Jesus is the Word of Scriptures (See John 5:39; Luke 24:27). Secondly, the word "testimony" means that God will do it again. This means that there is an anointing to see, do, and experience in God what has already been and what is yet to be seen, done, and experienced in God.

The Spirit of Prophecy is an invitation to experience God in the here and now by way of revelation. Truth is that there are various levels of revelation, which can serve to unlock a greater understanding in God's word. Revelation will also bring us into a greater intimacy with the Lord. In dealing with the Spirit of Prophecy we will learn different ways in which revelation is received such as through dreams and visions. This can also be considered a prophetic grace or revelatory anointing, speaking of that which empowers us prophetically.

What is a Prophetic Grace?

> Numbers 11:29
> And Moses said unto him, Enviest thou for my sake? would God that all the LORD'S people were prophets, and that the LORD would put his spirit upon them!

All cannot serve in the office of the prophet, but all can experience and function in the prophetic. In fact, one of the main functions of the prophetic office is to release and impart the prophetic grace.[1] It is the Spirit of prophecy that enables men who do not operate in the prophetic gifting or office to come under the same anointing of one who does. The reality is that the grace to function in the prophetic can only come by the sovereignty of God or by being connected to someone who can impart it.

Examples of the Prophetic Impartation:

<u>Saul</u>

> 1 Samuel 10:10-11
> (10) And when they came thither to the hill, behold, a company of prophets met him; and the Spirit of God came upon him, and he prophesied among them. (11) And it came to pass, when all that knew him beforetime saw that, behold, he prophesied among the prophets, then the people said one

to another, What is this that is come unto the son of Kish? Is Saul also among the prophets?

1 Samuel 19:20-24
(20) And Saul sent messengers to take David: and when they saw the company of the prophets prophesying, and Samuel standing as appointed over them, the Spirit of God was upon the messengers of Saul, and they also prophesied. (21) And when it was told Saul, he sent other messengers, and they prophesied likewise. And Saul sent messengers again the third time, and they prophesied also. (22) Then went he also to Ramah, and came to a great well that is in Sechu: and he asked and said, Where are Samuel and David? And one said, Behold, they be at Naioth in Ramah. (23) And he went thither to Naioth in Ramah: and the Spirit of God was upon him also, and he went on, and prophesied, until he came to Naioth in Ramah. (24) And he stripped off his clothes also, and prophesied before Samuel in like manner, and lay down naked all that day and all that night. Wherefore they say, Is Saul also among the prophets?

We have seen in first Samuel chapters ten and nineteen that the prophetic grace is transferable. For example, in the previous scripture reference, the Spirit of prophecy did not only cover the house where Samuel was, but it covered both the whole city and the surrounding areas. It was as if the prophetic anointing was air borne in that whole region, becoming contagious to anyone who would dare to come so close.

In other words, the anointing of God is so real and tangible that it can affect the very air we breathe. The prophetic anointing is "up for grabs". It is available to all of those who thirst after God to pour out His Spirit in their lives.

In 1 Samuel 19:22, we should also note that the prophetic came upon Saul at a well. This is significant because in those days a well was a public place much like a gas station or shopping center would be in our current culture. This is symbolic of how the Spirit of prophecy is not limited to church services.

We must remember that it is the testimony of Jesus (Revelations 19:10). This means that the prophetic should empower our witness and our sharing of the gospel to those who are yet to be saved. In this hour God is raising up a prophetic people who become powerful witnesses and evangelists. As we receive a prophetic grace to directly encounter God, we will be empowered to more effectively take our faith to the public. Now lets take a look at another example of prophetic impartation.

Gehazi

2 Kings 6:16-17
(16) And he answered, Fear not: for they that be with us are more than they that be with them. (17) And Elisha prayed, and said, LORD, I pray thee, open his eyes, that he may see. And the LORD opened the eyes of the young man; and he saw: and, behold, the mountain was full of horses and chariots of fire round about Elisha.

In the previous text, it was what Elisha saw in the Spirit that gave him great peace and boldness in a time of danger. However, Gehazi was not able to see what Elisha saw until after Elisha prayed that God would open his eyes. It was this prayer that became an impartation of the prophetic anointing.

The previous scriptural references of both Saul and Gehazi are examples of normal men coming under a prophetic grace and anointing through someone who occupied the prophetic office. Saul and Gehazi experienced the Spirit of prophecy just as any of us can. In fact, in the last days God has promised to pour out His Spirit on all flesh and cause us to prophesy (Acts 2:17).

This is That:
Acts 2:17
Understanding the Feast of Pentecost & The Upper Room

As we continue to define the Spirit of Prophecy it will help if we began to study within the context of when Pentecost began. As we do, we will discover that it had always been God's desire to bring all of His people into a direct encounter with Himself. We will also better understand Pentecost in the upper room as we understand the origin of Pentecost in the book of Exodus chapter twenty.

The Origin of Pentecost

Exodus 20:18-21
(18) And all the people saw the thunderings, and the lightnings, and the noise of the trumpet, and the mountain smoking: and when the people saw it, they removed, and stood afar off. (19) And they said unto Moses, Speak thou with us, and we will hear: but let not God speak with us, lest we die. (20) And Moses said unto the people, Fear not: for God is come to prove you, and that his fear may be before your faces, that ye sin not. (21) And the people stood afar off, and Moses drew near unto the thick darkness where God was.

The previous scripture has its context during the feast of Pentecost. The history of it is that in Exodus 19:6, God called the nation of Israel to what is called the Holy Mount in order to accept the ministry of the priesthood. Exodus 20:18-21 is actually the account of Israel's response to that priestly call.

The priesthood in one essence speaks of those who directly access the presence and glory of God. It is also interesting to note historically that it was the priesthood that prepared Samuel to embrace his prophetic office. This is significant in that it was Samuel who was the first prophet to establish the prophetic as an "official service" within Israel's structure of culture and government.

Simply put, the history of the prophetic is connected to the history of the priesthood, which is connected to the origin of Pentecost. Therefore a greater understanding of the prophetic is partially connected to a greater understanding of Pentecost.

When Israel rejected the priesthood, God began to use the Levitical priesthood instead. This meant that only the Levites could directly access the presence of the Lord and the sacred things in the temple. The day of Pentecost in the book of Acts is significant in that it was the exact season of time in which the Israelites rejected the presence of God (Exodus 20:18-21).

However, although Israel rejected the call as a kingdom of priests, when the time of Pentecost had fully come according to the Hebraic fiscal year, in the book of Acts God revisited His people to fulfill His original desire. During the first Pentecost at the mountain "only Moses drew" near, but during Pentecost in the upper room "all were filled."

Contrasting the Upper Room and the Holy Mount
There is some resemblance in the two experiences.

Upper room = they saw tongues of fire (Acts 2:3)

Holy mountain= they saw thunder (Ex 20:18)

There is a connection in the two Pentecostal experiences recorded in the books of Exodus and Acts. In fact, I believe that the experience of the disciples "seeing tongues of fire" in the upper room, and the experience of Israel "seeing thunder" at the holy mountain can be correlated. In order to grasp the connection of these two historical moments we should ask ourselves a couple questions as we examine the texts.

The first question we should ask is, how in the world did Israel see thunder? Secondly, we should ask ourselves, how is this connected to what happened in the upper room? The explanation is within the Hebraic definition for the word thunder.

In Exodus 20:18 the word thunder literally means "voices glorified in fire". I believe that the "tongues of fire" seen in the upper room could possibly be the same "voices glorified in fire" that God had originally desired to release to the Israelites in Exodus 20:18. This means that the experience at the mountain in the book of Exodus could be a type and shadow of the day of Pentecost in the book of acts.

It would also represent God always having a desire to call all people into His presence and fill us with His Spirit. This is significant because we will only receive a greater understanding of the prophetic as we also better understand the outpour of God's Spirit. Lets gp deeper.

Acts 2:16
But this is that which was spoken by the prophet Joel;

In Acts 2:17, Peter's answer to the mockers and scorners of the Pentecostal outpour was the declaration "this is that." In other words, this is what God intended from the beginning. All throughout scripture God signified that there would be a people in whom He would place His Spirit.

These people would be a prophetic people. It was not by chance that Peter stood to declare the prophetic word of Joel, which was nothing less than what God always desired for His people from the time they left Egypt. And just as it was with Israel, the benefits of a Pentecostal outpour is nothing less than what God wants for us to set us free from the bondages and the limitations of our present day Egypt, which is this present world. Let's take a closer look at what the Pentecostal outpour offers us and what connection it has to the prophetic.

Full Pentecost:

Acts 2:1-4
(1) And when the day of Pentecost was fully come, they were all with one accord in one place. (2) And suddenly there came a sound from heaven as of a rushing mighty wind, and it filled all the house where they were sitting. (3) And there appeared unto them cloven tongues like as of fire, and it sat upon each of them. (4) And they were all filled with the Holy Ghost, and began to speak with other tongues, as the Spirit gave them utterance.

- They heard a sound
- They saw tongues of fire
- They were filled and the Holy Spirit came upon them according to Acts 1:8
- They began to speak with tongues

The early church received a full thrust and submersion into the things of the Spirit or what is better known as the Baptism in the Holy Ghost. Their eyes, ears, mouths, and their bodies became receptive to the spirit realm around them. In fact, God wants all to see, hear, and experience Him in the supernatural at some level. This is called revelation as we have learned in chapter one.

It's almost impossible to separate speaking in tongues and prophesying from experiencing God in the supernatural. The reality is that we all can experience some level of revelation. In fact, revelation is the way that God empowers us to be in this world and yet not of this world. Without revelation it is impossible to live in this world and not conform to it (Romans 12:2). When God pours out His Spirit we start receiving dreams, visions, and various types of revelation. Our prayer lives are supercharged, we begin to demonstrate His power, and we begin to prophesy (Acts 2:16-18).

Joel 2:28
And it shall come to pass afterward, that I will pour out my spirit upon all flesh; and your sons and your daughters shall prophesy, your old men shall dream dreams, your young men shall see visions:

Last days = Spirit on all Flesh = Joel 2:28; Acts 2:16

> Spirit poured out
>
> Dreams and visions
>
> Prophecy and signs

According to Joel 2:28 and Acts 2:16, God's Spirit being poured out, dreams, visions, prophecy, signs and wonders are all common manifestations when God moves in the earth. They are the Spirit of Prophecy. They are the testimony of Jesus Christ. Also, according to the previous references, both the outpour of God's Spirit and the manifestations of the outpour are available to be experienced by "all flesh". Therefore, men and women both young and old can all see dreams, visions, signs, wonders, and begin to prophesy.

Many read the prophecy of Joel concerning the outpour and interpret well until they read the part about the old men and the young men. The scripture is not saying that only old men can dream while only young men can see visions. The distinctions of the manifestations listed in Joel 2:28 are only to "emphasize the context" and not to "exclude the experience".

We must remember that these prophetic encounters are available to everyone and they are released as God's Spirit is poured out on ALL flesh. In fact, the word "vision" in Joel 2:28 is defined as dream, vision, or revelation. Therefore, the correct interpretation of the text is that old and young alike can both see visions and dream dreams.

A great example of this is when Daniel spoke of the "vision of his dreams" (Daniel 4:9-10). Why didn't Daniel just call the vision a dream? The answer is that Daniel understood that he had no need to exclude a particular experience from the other because of how all manifestations of the prophetic are relative.

All of the manifestations of prophetic experience correlate and they are not exclusive to gender, race, or age. All can see visions and dreams. All can show signs and wonders after God's Spirit has been poured out upon them. All can experience various levels of revelation. There is an invitation and grace to experience God in the supernatural, speak the word of the Lord, and demonstrate the power of God. Through the Spirit of Prophecy we can experience the supernatural in revelation so that we can release the supernatural in demonstration.

Criteria for the Prophetic:

God's Spirit on all flesh is the criteria for all to come into prophetic experience according to the book of Joel. Revelation encounters have always been the standard of the prophetic. In fact, another definition for the word "vision" actually means divinely granted visitation.

A divinely granted visitation is when we entertain the direct audience of God. It is when we engage in revelatory experiences through the activation of all of our sensory capabilities (sight, smell, touch, hearing, taste). I will expound upon this in more detail over the next chapter, but for now just think about this. How else can we prophesy unless we have experienced God? The Old Testament prophets are our examples.

The Old Testament prophets are our example:

Hebrews 1:1
God, who at sundry times and in divers manners spake in time past unto the fathers by the prophets,

According to Hebrews 1:1 God spoke to the prophets in "divers manners". In other words, the prophets would experience various levels of revelation and divine communication. They interacted with God in a diversity of ways to receive the messages that they were to deliver to God's people.

Examples:

Habakkuk 2:1 messages through visions

Ezekiel 3:14-15 messages given in outer body experiences

Daniel 9:21-22 messages through angels

* For too long the prophetic has been limited to "thus saith the Lord." Prophetic revelation is yet received in many different ways. The prophetic is not always released through "thus saith the Lord." In fact, thus saith the Lord is something that happens, not just something we say. It was something that signified the Lord literally speaking through the Prophet and using his mouth supernaturally. When this would take place, even the prophet himself wouldn't know what he was saying until after he had heard himself already speaking it. Even this is only one dynamic of revelatory flow that the prophet experiences. How else can we prophesy unless we have experienced God? *

Revelation is the very source of the prophetic. It is the very Spirit of prophecy and the essence of what it means to experience God in the supernatural. Over the next chapter we will articulate and expound upon various levels of revelation in great detail.

Chapter 3

Spirit of Prophecy:

Levels of Prophetic Revelation

"May be able to comprehend with all saints what is the breadth, and length, and depth, and height; And to know the love of Christ which passeth knowledge, that ye might be filled with all the fullness of God." Ephesians 3:18-19

Key Points:
- Understand more specifically what it actually means to experience God in the supernatural by defining what prophetic revelation is
- Continue to understand the spirit of prophecy
- Understand multiple levels of prophetic revelation
- Discern and embrace over 21 ways that God Interacts and Communicates with all believers as follows: Impressions, dreams, visions, levels & degrees of seeing in the Spirit, trances, outer body experiences, God's audible voice, angelic encounters, visitations of Jesus, and more
- Understand how to stir up, activate, and access revelation: Embracing God Encounters

Getting Activated in Revelation:

If you have made it to this chapter it means that you have crossed the foundational threshold and you are ready to be activated into revelation. Understanding the prophetic and its many different dimensions has helped us in understanding the supernatural. However, now that the foundation has been laid, it is also important we know that there is a difference between understanding the supernatural and experiencing it.

The spirit of prophecy is a realm of the prophetic by which we actually experience God through various forms of revelations from which is derived the phrase "prophetic revelation". Hebrews 1:1 teaches that God interacts with the prophets in a diversity of ways (divers manners). In the same way, not only does God interact with His prophets, but He also deals with all believers prophetically in a diversity of ways through various levels of revelation.

This teaching is designed to expose you to various types and degrees of supernatural experience and show how this is available to all believers. In this chapter we will distinguish the different levels of prophetic revelation and in doing so we will begin to understand what it means to actually experience God in the supernatural. The following scripture teaches us why it is important to learn and embrace the various different ways that God may choose to interact with us as believers.

> Philemon 1:6
> That the communication of thy faith may become effectual by the acknowledging of every good thing which is in you in Christ Jesus.

Based upon the previous text, awareness and recognition is key in not only understanding the prophetic, but also actually benefiting from the access we have into supernatural realms of prophetic revelation. In other words, we will either be propelled or hindered in what God is doing in our lives depending on how we are able and willing to acknowledge and cooperate with what is taking place.

Teaching concerning the supernatural is therefore imperative because it is as we recognize the prophetic and become more aware of the supernatural that we literally cultivate an atmosphere to engage and grow in revelatory and prophetic experience.[1] As you continue to read an impartation can released causing you to experience the information that you have embraced. As you study the following teaching I prophesy that the heavens are opening over your life. God's Spirit is being poured out on your flesh and the glory of God is being manifested.

Whenever the Lord opens the heavens, pours out of His Spirit, or when His Glory is seen, revelation is guaranteed to proceed. For instance, it was when the Glory of God was seen that the heavens opened and revelation was given to Ezekiel through visions, angelic messengers, and visitations of the Lord (Ezekiel 1:1, 28). It is also when the Lord pours out of His Spirit that Joel signified that all flesh begins to experience prophetic revelation all inclusive of visions, dreams, signs, and wonders (Joel 2:28-32). This is the time for dreams, visions, signs, wonders, and the like. May this chapter and the remainder of this book be as a tool to activate you therein.

Visions & Revelations: Classifying Revelatory Experience

The word "vision" is the most common word used to describe prophetic revelation other than the word "prophecy" in both the New and Old Testaments. For example, at times Paul would refer to the personal appearances of the Lord Jesus he encountered as revelations and at other times he referred to them as visions.[1] Likewise, most of the prophets who encountered the Lord in the Old Testament also referred to their experiences as a vision.

Simply put, a vision is a revelation and a revelation is a vision. In fact, the word "vision" and the word "revelation" are both inclusive of multiple ways that God interacts with us as His people. This truth covers a host of spiritual dynamics.

Visions have a vast category of revelatory experience ranging from the seemingly unaware to the dramatic. They can be either internal or external revelations. The revelations can also be pictorial, panoramic, and even interactive.

Visions can consist of various glimpses into the heavens, supernaturally screened motioned images, or even divine encounters with the Lord. They are obviously inclusive of multiple different levels of prophetic revelation. And as we examine these levels of revelation we will obtain clarity on the ways that God interacts and communicates with us as believers.

The key in understanding a biblical study on revelatory experiences is to be as precise as possible in defining and understanding biblical terminology. We must balance and compare the original definitions of the words we study with adequate scriptural references of actual experiences in order to understand spiritual truths concerning prophetic revelation. For example, a revelatory experience is sometimes identified scripturally by the state a person is in while receiving the revelation instead of being identified as actual revelation itself. Dreams, slumbering, trances, and meditations are adequate references of this truth. A great example of this is found in Job 33:14-15.

> Job 33:14-15
> For God speaketh once, yea twice, yet man perceiveth it not. (15) In a dream, in a vision of the night, when deep sleep falleth upon men, in slumberings upon the bed;

In the previous text three different states of unconsciousness are referenced as follows: dreams, slumbering, and deep sleep. We can scripturally conclude that, "Godly dreams" are visions and revelations that take place in our sleep. Slumbering is more descriptive of when a person is half awake and half sleep. Deep sleep is actually symbolic of "trances" in the Old Testament in which we will cover in detail later in this chapter.

The point is that the three examples in the book of Job are more descriptive of the state a person may go into in order to receive a vision or revelation. In addition to this, there is a host of scriptural linguistics pertaining to the prophetic. The following chart is consists of different terminologies that were descriptive of revelatory experiences throughout the history of the prophetic that can help us classify levels of revelation.

Brief History of Prophetic Revelation: Clarity in Terminology

Moses = dreams, similitude, visions (appearances)
(Numbers 12:6-8)
Samuel = visions and appearances
(Samuel 3:1, 7, 10, 21)
Ezekiel = visions of God
(Ezekiel 1:1)
Joel = dreams and visions
(Joel 2:28)
Hosea = visions and similitude
(Hosea 12:10)
Paul = visions and revelations (appearances)
(2 Corinthians 12:1-4)
John = spirit of prophecy
(Revelations 19:10)

The prophetic, visions, revelation, similitude, and dreams, as listed in the previous chart, are all synoptic. They all come forth of the same essence and reality. A great example of this is found when Joel mentions dreams and visions in Joel 2:28.

In the book of Joel the word "vision" literally means vision, dream, and revelation. We can therefore conclude that "visions and revelations" mentioned by the Apostle Paul must be understood within the context of the "dreams and visions" spoken of by the Prophet Joel. Let's not forget also the mentioning of similitudes by the prophet Hosea, which all should be understood in context of what John embraced to be the Spirit of prophecy. Each previous example speaks pertaining to different levels and classifications of prophetic revelation.

For some, this truth may be difficult to grasp because unlike the apostles and prophets of old, our understanding and ideas of revelation are usually narrow and vague. In fact, there are seven Hebraic variations of the word "vision" in the Old Testament, each one conveying various aspects of prophetic revelation. Furthermore, each of the seven variations for the word "vision" can fall under one of the three classifications as follows: basic visions, open visions, and visitations/appearances.

I have discovered that the seven variations for the word vision can be narrowed down into the previous three categories because of how some of the definitions are closely associated. Therefore, the categories will be the foundation by which we study and expound upon multiple different levels of prophetic revelation. As we look at the different classifications of visions and other revelations, keep in mind that these categories are neither exclusive nor limited to our present or any future level of knowledge.

As you study, you should keep in mind that many who teach on the prophetic may articulate various levels of prophetic revelation differently. It does not matter if the articulation is unique as long as the interpretation is the same. I personally chose to articulate revelatory experiences accordingly so that I could adequately reference word study and scripture references as we progressively advance in our studies. As we expound upon various revelatory encounters and visionary experiences within the following three classifications, we will discover

over twenty-one ways that God may choose to interact with or communicate with us as believers at any given time.

Experiencing God in the Supernatural
Levels of Revelation:
(Basic Visions, Open Visions, and Visitations/Appearances)
Similitudes: Basic level Visions

Hosea 12:10
I have also spoken by the prophets, and I have multiplied visions, and used similitudes, by the ministry of the prophets.

Hosea 12 is speaking of visions and similitudes in the prophetic, which is the first category from which I will expound upon levels of revelation. Although the word "similitude" stands apart from the word "vision" in this particular verse, we must understand that the word "similitude" is actually one of the definitions for the word "vision" in the Hebraic language. It is in fact one of the more consistent definitions among the seven variations for the word vision, which is the reason that I choose to define this word first as a foundation to categorize revelatory experience and explain what a basic level vision consists of.

This word "similitude" according to our text in Hosea has to do with the inner dealings of God by definition. Its definition and its root word denote thought, imagery, and even silence. A great working definition for the word could be as follows: a thought that impresses the likeness or knowledge of God upon the heart.

Similitudes are often articulated as being impressions, spontaneous thought, perceptions, intuition, and etc. among many prophetic companies in modern day church culture. This level of revelation is the most frequent and often most ignored way that God speaks to the believer. A similitude mostly refers to what happens when God apprehends the spirit or the soul of man.

This means that God can show us a vision without our natural eyes being able to see what He is showing us. He impresses a vision upon our hearts and leaves us with the picture of a reality that exists beyond what our natural eyes can see. This is called an imagination. It has the power to alter our outlook on life and cause us to see things from God's perspective.

God will frequently deal with us in ways that require us to develop our spiritual perception and sensitivity (Job 33:14). The ability to perceive things by the Spirit of God is the ability to receive Divine information into our spirits and afterwards progressively process it into our minds and actions. We will examine this truth in more detail later in this chapter. A Similitude can include impressions, unction, or what Daniel called the visions in his head, which are often also considered to be "closed visions" among many prophetic companies.

Daniel 4:5
I saw a dream which made me afraid, and the thoughts upon my bed and the visions of my head troubled me.

The visions spoken of by Daniel in Daniel 4:5 were pictorial messages in his head. What Daniel saw were in fact visions, but because God was dealing with him inwardly it should be categorized as a similitude and more specifically in this case articulated as an inner or closed vision.

Three Aspects of a Similitude

1. Counsels of the Heart: a divine knowing or fixing of the heart by a series of thought

How does this work?

Proverbs 16:1-3
The <u>preparations of the heart</u> in man, and the answer of the tongue, is from the LORD (2) All the ways of a man are clean in his own eyes; but the LORD <u>weigheth the spirits</u>. (3) Commit thy works unto the LORD, and thy <u>thoughts shall be established</u>. (See also Proverbs 21:1-2)

The preparations of the heart, the weighing of our spirits, and the establishing of our thoughts are all dealing with the inner man in the above scripture. Now let's look at two key words in the text above that will help us understand the inward dealings of God in man. The two words are as follows: weigheth and pndereth.

The word "weigheth" in Proverbs sixteen and the word "pondereth" in Proverbs twenty-one are both the same word in the original language. Both words mean to examine, test, establish, arrange, level, or direct. Not only does God "examine" our hearts, but at times God will apprehend our minds in order to "counsel" our hearts. When this happens God touches our spirits in a way that causes a certain thought to cross our minds. After this, it is as if we cannot "shake" this thought as the Holy Spirit continues for a period of time to bring this thought to our remembrance (John 14:26). Hearing God's voice is as easy as receiving one Holy Spirit inspired thought that keeps processing repeatedly in our minds.[1]

2. <u>Impressions/Perceptions:</u> a divine knowing by a conscience sense of the anointing bringing illumination and awareness. To perceive or have intuition by which "YOU JUST KNOW!" Sometimes you don't know how you know, but all of a sudden you just know.[1]

How does this work?

> Mark 2:8
> And immediately when Jesus perceived in his spirit that they so reasoned within themselves, he said unto them, Why reason ye these things in your hearts? (See also Luke 5:22).

In Mark 2:8, Jesus perceived in His spirit or His innermost being. Perception allows us to come into an understanding and knowledge of a particular matter while bypassing the natural process of comprehension. This is possible because our spirits can register information and communication quicker and more accurately than our brains.

In the natural, information is processed when certain nerves communicate messages back and forth from the brain and the body's functioning organs and senses. An impression is instead the communication of God's Spirit into our spirits. This type of revelation rather communicates information that is processed in our spirit man, but it is only discerned if our inner/spirit man is renewed daily.

This level of revelation is only discerned if our inner man is renewed

2 Corinthians 4: 16, 18
…but though our outward man perish, yet the inward man is renewed day by day. (18) while we look not at the things which are seen, but at the things which are not seen….

There are two keys according to the previous scriptures concerning our spirit man being renewed. First, our outward man must perish. Secondly, our focus must be on spiritual things. As we die to our flesh by humility, fasting, and prayer we allow our spirit man (which is considered to be the inner man/the new man) the opportunity to be strengthened and renewed. According to 2 Corinthians 4:16-18 and Colossians 3:10, this is a daily process in which the word of God is imperative.

Colossians 3:10
And have put on the "new man", which is <u>renewed in knowledge</u> after the image of him that created him:

Anything we receive in the Holy Ghost is first transmitted in our inner most being. God deals with our spirit man and then it registers in our mind. The stronger our spirits are the more we can perceive things in the Holy Ghost.

First, it is our knowledge in the word of God that renews the strength of our spirit man. Next, it is then the strength of our spirit man that develops a keen sensitivity. Lastly, as we continue to develop sensitivity to truth and God realities by spending time in the word of God, we will begin to notice the slightest dealings and promptings of God. This has a lot to do with the renewing of our mind, which is a powerful truth that we will expound upon in the coming pages.

The Holy Spirit is assigned to deal with us in the context of Truth

John 14:17, 26
Even the Spirit of truth; whom the world cannot receive, because it seeth him not, neither knoweth him: but ye know him; for he dwelleth with you, and shall be in you. (26) Even

the Spirit of truth; whom the world cannot receive, because it seeth him not, neither knoweth him: but ye know him; for he dwelleth with you, and shall be in you.

1 John 2:27
But the anointing which ye have received of him abideth in you, and ye need not that any man teach you: but as the same anointing teacheth you of all things, and is truth, and is no lie, and even as it hath taught you, ye shall abide in him.

According to 1 John 2:27 and John 14:17, 26, the anointing and the Spirit of God will always deal with us within the context of "truth". This means that spending time in the word and in the presence of the Lord develops our sensitivity to Holy Ghost perception. The more we recognize and heed God's voice in the word, the more we will recognize His voice within this level of revelation.

If our character and our spirits are not in line with the scriptures we can be sure that our perception is either wrong or coming from an illegal source. This realm of revelation can prove to be a transmitter of very accurate and precise information and should be developed along with character and accountability (Matthew 7:15-16). Let me explain why with an awareness of the fact that you may have to take this into careful thought and consideration.

These levels of revelation deal more with our ability to perceive rather than God's ability to speak. Therefore, our own spirits can be misleading if we are not truly submitted to the Lord Jesus. We must spend time in the word of God and in prayer to be sure that we are accurately and properly engaging this realm of the supernatural. If we will know God's voice in this realm we must be sure we are constantly renewing our minds.

Renewing the Mind

There is an amazing truth concerning the renewing of our minds that I believe many over look. The key word is "renew". Truth is that it is impossible to renew anything about our minds that was not already present at one point. This means that we already know what we need to know and our spirits already understand what we need to understand.

Our spirits are like eternal hard drives that are constantly receiving data downloads through the Holy Ghost of things pertaining to the past, present, and the future according 1 Corinthians 2:11-12. At any given moment we could access heaven's library similar to how Moses and Paul did when God allowed them to see eternity's past, before time began, concerning how He initiated creation (Genesis 1&2;Colossians 1:16-17).

At other times revelation will cause our spirits to act as a satellite radar tower, able to scan and detect the most intricate facts and details of the present. Elijah functioned in this capacity, as he was able to hear and see into the privacy of the king's chamber.

There are also times when revelation comes to cause us to function as a human GPS navigational system automatically programed to know what direction to take. Joseph is a great example of how revelation assists us in critical decision-making. He was able to interpret a dream that guided a whole nation for a succeeding fourteen-year period. The Lord has designed that His Spirit reveals these types of things to us, yet if our minds are not renewed we cannot partake of this benefit.

We should also understand concerning the renewing of our mind that we have both a conscious mind and a subconscious mind. Hebrews 10:22 speaks of our conscious mind. However, Ephesians 4:23 speaks of our subconscious mind when it talks about the "spirit of our mind".

It is the spirit of our mind, which is our subconscious mind that needs to be renewed through the word of God. The word "sub" means under. This means that although our subconscious mind has the ability to receive knowledge, understanding, and wisdom through the Holy Ghost, it often remains suppressed. It is our job to reteach our minds what our spirits already know.

The word of God can so sharpen our spiritual perception that we will begin to discern and know things beyond our natural comprehension. It will cause us to have a conscious awareness of things that only the Holy Ghost could make known (Hebrews 4:12). If we will get in the Holy Ghost and get in the word of God, the Lord will begin to reveal knowledge, understanding, and wisdom that is beyond this world.

3. Dark Speeches /Hard Sentences:

> Numbers 12:6-8
> And he said, Hear now my words: If there be a prophet among you, I the LORD will make myself known unto him in a vision, and will speak unto him in a dream. (7)My servant Moses is not so, who is faithful in all mine house. (8)With him will I speak mouth to mouth, even apparently, and not in <u>dark speeches</u>; and the similitude of the LORD shall he behold: wherefore then were ye not afraid to speak against my servant Moses.

> Daniel 5:12
> Forasmuch as an excellent spirit, and knowledge, and understanding, interpreting of dreams, and <u>shewing of hard sentences</u>, and dissolving of doubts, were found in the same Daniel, whom the king named Belteshazzar: now let Daniel be called, and he will shew the interpretation.

Other types of similitudes include dark speeches and hard sentences, which are simply illustrative messages. They speak of things that are revealed by comparison, resemblance, and symbolism. They often carry hidden pictorial messages and need to be interpreted.

The word teaches us in first Corinthians chapter two that the Holy Spirit teaches us by "comparing" spiritual things. This means that the language of the Spirit can be often symbolic. Therefore, we should not discredit the dealings of God just because we don't understand initially.

Dark speeches are very frequent in dreams. They are also administered within closed visions, daydreams, visualization, parables or the imagination. They need to be properly translated in order for a message to be conveyed and accurately articulated.

More about Similitudes:

We must become more aware of when God apprehends our minds or prompt our hearts. We cannot afford to ignore or misinterpret our inner convictions. A lot of times we want to see and hear but we're looking with the wrong eye or hearing with the wrong ear (Ezekiel 3:10).

When we learn to hear God, we learn to see with the eyes of our heart (Ephesians 1:17-18). Similitudes train, tune, and develop our spirit/inner sensitivity. A proper resolve, even for those who are mature, is to have accountability in our lives and be submitted to a continual developing of character and experience. As I for-mentioned, these levels of revelation deal more with our developing ability to perceive rather than God's ability to speak.

It is only as we spend time in the presence of the Lord and renewing our minds in the word of God that we develop keen sensitivity in discerning the dealings of God within these levels of revelation. This concludes the three types of similitudes, which are as follows: counsels of the heart, impressions/perceptions, and dark speeches/hard sentences. The next levels of revelation to understand are "open visions", but first lets take time to review other "inner dealings" of God on the following chart that are designed to bring about an awareness that the Lord is making impressions upon our hearts.

<u>Other Inner Dealings of God: Personal Study</u>

Trembling
(Job 4:14; Genesis 15:12; Daniel 10:7)

Zoned-Intense Focus
(Acts 11:6)

Inward Stirring; Bubbling Forth
(Jeremiah 20:9; John 7:37)

Peace
(Isaiah 30:15; Philippians 4:7; Matthew 11:28-30)

Joy
(Ephesians 5:7-11; Jeremiah 15:16)

Conviction
(John 15:7-11; Romans 2:15)

B. Open Visions: 2nd classification

Vision = looking glasses; seen with the eye.

Another variation for the word "vision" is defined as looking glasses or something seen through the natural eye. Open visions are the second classification of visionary experiences as pertaining to levels of prophetic revelation. An open vision has a lot to do with the ability to see spiritual things through the natural eye and much more.

Open visions occur when God takes the scales from our eyes allowing us to see the existence or activity of that which is behind the scenes in the Spiritual realm. Another definition of the word vision is a revelation through clear visual communication. The following scripture is a great example of this.

> Habakkuk 2:1
> I will stand upon my watch, and set me upon the tower, and will watch to see what he will say unto me, and what I shall answer when I am reproved.

In the previous scripture, Habakkuk says that he would "watch to see" what God would "say" to him. In other words God would give the message to him through visual communication. This means that at times God allows us to see things as a form of communication.

We have heard it said that a picture is worth a thousand words and this statement is very true when it comes to the spiritual dynamics of an open vision. In fact, as people we really don't think in words, but we do think in pictures. For example, children learn pictures, shapes, and colors as fundamentals and as they grow older words are connected to the pictures to add meaning.

As it is in the natural so it is in the spiritual. God will at times show us things in the Spirit that represent a fundamental foundation of understanding for the message He is conveying by revelation. At other times God allows us to see not because there is a prophetic message involved, but for the purpose of being aware and properly gauging the atmosphere around us. Great examples are the appearances of shapes, lights, angelic manifestations, glory manifestations, smoke, fire, clouds, and the like.

Levels and Degrees of Seeing in the Spirit

At times visions come in the glimpses, almost like a camera snap shot. It's there for a moment and before you know it, it's gone. We should understand that although our conscious awareness of the vision was brief, our spirits have the capacity to process information faster than our brains. Therefore, as we tune in by simply focusing on what we remember of the vision, God will allow us to retrieve the information that was branded on our spirits when delivered by way of the vision.

When this happens we will either have a divine knowing and understanding of the message that God has given, or God will simply show us more. We don't always understand what God is showing the first time around. This is why after God gives us a vision we must invest time and interest in what He has shown during the process of the vision becoming plain (Habakkuk 2:2-3).

Scripture teaches that we are to incline our ear toward understanding. This is why when Moses saw the burning bush in the wilderness; the scripture says that he "turned aside" to "see". The burning bush that Moses initially saw would have meant nothing to him if he had decided not to focus his attention on what God was showing him.

God showed Moses the burning bush in order to grab his attention and afterward gave Moses more revelation as he paid attention to the first revelation. Jesus taught an amazing truth concerning how to receive revelation in Mark 4:23. If we study closely what Jesus taught in the book of Mark chapter four we learn some amazing truths.

Jesus first of all tells us to take heed to both how things are revealed and what is actually being revealed. He then goes on to say that whoever would take heed would develop more of an ability to receive revelation and would have a more consistent flow of revelation in their lives. The previous truth is illustrated perfectly in Acts 11:4-10 as Peter expounds on the vision God had given him in a trance concerning preaching the gospel to the gentile nations. We see clearly in verse four that God gave Peter a vision, yet according to verse five it was only as Peter "fastened his eyes to consider" that God showed him more.

Visions can begin as glimpses or random spontaneous thoughts, yet if we will tune into God there is more to be seen. When this happens, visions can progress into a more panoramic type of view similar to what happened to Peter. This degree of visionary experience is more graphic and detailed in both what we see and in the nature of how the vision unfolds before our eyes.

What Peter saw in the trance could be equivalent to a motion picture trailer with digital Dolby surround sound. Although this is very intriguing and graphic, there is yet another stage of seeing in the Spirit where visions become what I liken to be as virtual reality. In these types of visions you actually feel as if you are in the vision as opposed to merely seeing the vision.

Not only do you feel as if you are in the vision but your senses are more enhanced to see, hear, taste, touch, or smell in the vision more so than your ability to see, hear, smell and etc. in the natural. Everything is enhanced because of how the vision allows us to taste a glimpse of heaven's reality. Time adjusts to eternity and even travel can take place at the speed of light.

A great example of the previous truth is found in Acts 12:6-11 in which an angel had come to rescue Peter out of prison. The scripture says that when Peter had come to himself after his rescue he thought that the whole experience was a vision. This means that Peter was most likely accustomed to experiencing visions in ways that felt similar to virtual reality or even natural reality.

Another great example is when Paul experienced a vision in which he traveled into paradise or when Ezekiel was given a scroll to eat in a vision that was sweet to his taste and yet bitter to his stomach. Even Ezekiel would travel to different locations within a vision, while Paul saw things that he could not explain. We will explain this more as we expound upon what Holy visitations are in the coming pages, but first lets deal with a degree of seeing in the Spirit that often goes unmentioned.

One degree of seeing in the Spirit that is more common among prophetic vessels is when God allows us to see into the Spirit realm. It is yet a completely different degree of seeing in the Spirit when we are allowed to see in the natural realm something that has manifested out of the spiritual realm. People often call this phenomenon.

Appearances of phenomenon can come in glimpses as well such as the appearances of lights, shapes, orbs, smoke vapors and such like. I have seen such glimpses especially pertaining to silhouettes of angels. A great way to describe these silhouettes of angels is the appearance of a transparent human shape.

At times I have seen silhouettes of angelic beings that look similar to how an invisible man special effects image would look in a movie. Their vibrations also often appear as the visible heat waves would appear on a hot sunny day. A great example of this is when Moses and the seventy elders beheld the form of God in the mountain. They saw the transparent shape of God's person but were not allowed to see His face.

Such appearances of phenomenon can also come to us more blatant in nature. Scriptures teach that in the last days there will be signs in the heavens and wonders in the earth. Great examples of this is how all of Israel would see a visible Glory cloud and pillars of fire leading them daily throughout the wilderness for the space of forty years.

Could you imagine how they would see a visible Glory cloud expanded over their heads until at night when it would shape shift into a visible fire. Or what about when David and multiple others saw the angel of the Lord standing in between heaven and earth with a sword in his hand at the threshing floor of Ornan in 1 Chronicles 21:16-20.

Lets' not forget about when the Babylonian king saw a visible hand writing an unknown language on his dining room wall in Daniel 5:5, or when at least one hundred and twenty witnesses watched Jesus levitate in the sky until a cloud received Him and escorted Him back into the heavens in Acts 1:9-10, 15. This may seem rare at the present time in which we live but scripture has promised that this will become more widespread in the last days. People will begin to see things that are either divinely or demonically inspired that will not necessarily require them having an ability to see into the spirit realm. This degree of seeing will cause things to appear before our eyes whether we are ready or not, yet it is still wise to develop our sensitivity in perceiving the revelations and visions of God.

C. Holy Visitation:

Visitation is the third classification of visionary experiences and levels of prophetic revelation. Another variation for the word vision is defined as divinely granted visitations.

A visitation is when visions become interactive beyond just the visual senses. In a visitation not only can we see, but we can also smell, touch, taste, hear, and even travel as we have previously become aware of. A great example of this is in Psalm 34:8 when the psalmist said that we are to taste and see that the Lord is good.

The word taste in the Hebrew actually means to experience with all of the senses. This means that we can literally experience the reality of God and the spirit world called heaven within the same capacity that we experience life on earth. The things of heaven can become unbelievably tangible in the earth.

Likewise, in a similar aspect we can access the heavenlies in a tangible way. Next, we will cover four types of visitations, which include ascending into the heavens, translations, open appearances and interactions of the Divine and the Lord Jesus Himself.

Ascending into the Heavens

Prophetic visions and revelation can become so tangible and interactive that they can include ascending into the heavens. Both Paul and John in the New Testament had experiences in which they were caught up into the heavens. The Bible teaches we can taste the powers of the world to come (Hebrews 6:5). Scriptures also teach that it is possible to see the land of heaven before transitioning there eternally (Isaiah 33:17). The following scriptures are great examples:

> 2 Corinthians 12:1-4
> It is not expedient for me doubtless to glory. I will come to visions and revelations of the Lord. **(2)** I knew a man in Christ above fourteen years ago, (whether in the body, I cannot tell; or whether out of the body, I cannot tell: God

knoweth;) such an one caught up to the third heaven. **(3)**And I knew such a man, (whether in the body, or out of the body, I cannot tell: God knoweth;) **(4)**How that he was caught up into paradise, and heard unspeakable words, which it is not lawful for a man to utter.

Revelations 4:1-2
After this I looked, and, behold, <u>a door was opened in heaven</u>: and <u>the first voice which I heard</u> was as it were of a trumpet talking with me; which <u>said, Come up hither</u>, and I will show thee things which must be hereafter. (2) <u>And immediately I was in the spirit: and, behold, a throne was set in heaven, and one sat on the throne.</u>

Ascending: The Basis of Heavenly Revelation

Simply put we can ascend because the heavens are open to us (Ezekiel 1:1; Isaiah 64:1-2; John 3:13; Ephesians 2:6)

John 3:13
And no man hath ascended up to heaven, but he that came down from heaven, even the Son of man which is in heaven.

Jesus spoke an amazing truth in John 3:13. He literally said in this verse that not only was He from heaven, but also although He came to the earth He had always existed eternally in Heavenly places. And because of this, although He was physically in the earth, He could still access the heavens.

The bible speaks the same of us as believers. Although we are physically in the earth we are also seated in heavenly places according to Ephesians 2:6. We can access heaven experientially because we have already been positioned and seated there spiritually as a result of our faith in Jesus as our Lord.

This is what made it possible for both Enoch and Elijah to be caught up and transported by the Spirit of God into Heaven. They were already positioned in heaven spiritually before they arrived to heaven physically. I know that was deep, but think about it again.

Two biblical experiences show men who experienced heaven and came back into the earth before death. Two other biblical experiences show men who were taken to heaven and now remain there eternally without even experiencing death. And remember that two or three witnesses establishes every word.

Therefore, to claim that one cannot experience heaven except through death is not biblical. Jesus has risen and ascended into the heavens. And according to the scriptures we have already risen, spiritually speaking, and have ascended to be positioned with Jesus even though we are awaiting the physical manifestation of our bodies ascending at the Lord's second coming (Ephesians 2:5- 6; Colossians 2:12-13; 3:1-4).[1] It is because of the previous scriptural facts that we can ascend into the heights of Zion and be caught up into the throne room and other third heaven encounters.

3 Other types of Visitations

1. Visitations of the Lord

Paul is a great example of one who experienced the visitations of the Lord. There are four definite biblical records of Jesus appearing to Paul. In fact, Jesus promised Paul in the scripture continual visitations beyond his initial encounter with the Lord at Damascus (Acts 26:16). Paul was personally taught and assisted in ministry by Jesus after the resurrection (See Galatians 1:11-12), because Jesus promised that He would manifest Himself after His resurrection according to John 14:19-21. And by the way, the word "manifest" in John 14:19-21 means to openly appear.

> 1 Corinthians 9:1
> …have not I seen Jesus Christ our Lord….

Paul's Visitations of Jesus

Acts 26:16 "clarity at Damascus; continual visitations promised"

Acts 18:9 "at Corinth"

Acts 22:17-18 "at Jerusalem before ministry"

Acts 23:11 "at Jerusalem after ministry"

Acts 26:16
But rise, and stand upon thy feet: for <u>I have appeared unto thee for this purpose</u>, to make thee a minister and a witness both of these things which thou hast seen, <u>and of those things in the which I will appear unto thee</u>;

There are also other indefinite biblical records of Jesus visiting Paul which are listed as follows for personal study:

(1 Corinthians 11:24-25; 2 Corinthians 12:7-9)

"Both Paul and Ezekiel would at times experience extended seasons of prophetic revelation." The intensity and abundance of the visions and revelations included visitations of the Lord, Angels, translations, and even ascending into heavenly encounters.

Examples:

2 Corinthians 12:1, 7
It is not expedient for me doubtless to glory. <u>I will come to visions and revelations</u> of the Lord. **(7)**And lest I should be exalted above measure through <u>the abundance of the revelations</u>, there was given to me a thorn in the flesh, the messenger of Satan to buffet me, lest I should be exalted above measure.

Ezekiel 1:1
Now it came to pass in the thirtieth year, in the fourth month, in the fifth day of the month, as I was among the

captives ᶠ¹ by the river of Chebar, that <u>the heavens were opened, and I saw</u> visions of God.

Notice the plural form of the words "vision" and "revelation" in 2 Corinthians 12:1, 7 and Ezekiel 1:1. It is one thing to have "a vision", but it is a completely different thing to have an abundance of visions and revelations, or like Ezekiel to be taken into a series of visions of God. The point is that heavenly encounters are not out of the norm for the Spirit filled believer. There is a grace over the body of Christ to bring us into not only an encounter, but also a series of prophetic revelations and encounters.

Visitations of the Lord Continued:

Paul was not the only person who saw Jesus after the resurrection. Visitations are one of the means that the Lord continues to work along with us today according to Mark 16:20. Review the following examples of others who experienced visitations of the Lord.

Acts 1:3
> To whom also he shewed himself alive after his passion by many infallible proofs, <u>being seen of them forty days</u>, and speaking of the things pertaining to the kingdom of God:

A. The disciple Ananias

> Acts 9:10-16
> Vs.10 And there was a certain disciple at Damascus, named Ananias; and to him said the Lord in a vision, Ananias. And he said, Behold, I am here, Lord.

B. Stephen the deacon

> Acts 7:55
> But he, being full of the Holy Ghost, looked up stedfastly into heaven, and saw the glory of God, and Jesus standing on the right hand of God.

Note: Stephen was so full of the Holy Ghost at this point that he was able to look into the heavens and see Jesus. Stephen saw Jesus in an open vision.

C John the apostle

Revelations 1:12-18
Vs. 12-13 And I turned to see the voice that spake with me. And being turned, I saw seven golden candlesticks; And in the midst of the seven candlesticks one like unto the Son of man......

2. Visitation of Angels

In addition to the visitations of the Lord Jesus Himself, another type of visitation is the visitation of angels. Angelic activity is not just an Old Testament occurrence. In fact, as we expound upon why and how angels function in chapter five, we will discover that their activities could be considered as rather normal in the world that we live in. Jesus had the assistance of angels throughout His time on earth and in His ministry (John 1:50-51). The early church also had the assistance of angels while the New Testament scriptures prophetically guarantee the increase of angelic activity throughout the end of this age.

We should understand that visitations, whether they are from the Lord or His angels, are not merely appearances, but they can also prove to be rather very interactive encounters just as described in scripture. For example, Jacob had a visitation so real in which he actually physically wrestled with the Lord (Genesis 32:24, 30). Abraham had a visitation in which he conversed with the Lord and two angels over dinner in Genesis chapter eighteen.

In Genesis chapter nineteen, Lot and his family experienced a visitation in which two angels physically spent the night in their house. Elijah had a visitation in which an angel came to him twice in the same day awaking him out of his sleep and preparing him food to eat (1 Kings 19:5-8). Visitations (a type of vision) of the Lord and angels are clearly not just figments of our imagination.

3. Visions and Translations

Translations are another type of visitation, which actually consists of us doing the visiting instead of the Lord and His angels. Translations are a means of supernatural travel, which can be instant or at an accelerated pace. They are possible because there is no time or distance in the realm of the spirit. Translations can also take place both within and out of the body (Isaiah 41:3). They can be both vertical and horizontal. A vertical translation is when a person whether in or out-of-the-body ascends into the heavens. A horizontal translation is when a person whether in or out-of-the-body is transported by the Holy Ghost into different parts of the earth.

Translations, especially in-the-body translations, in most cases are a very rare occurrence. There are only two vertical-in-the-body translations mentioned in scripture after Pentecost. One is the rapture, which scripturally known as the "catching away" of the believers in the sky to meet the Lord. The other is that of the two prophets that God sends during the days of tribulation. There is only one horizontal-in-the-body translation mentioned in scripture after Pentecost, which is pertaining to Philip the deacon and evangelist. The following is a great scripture reference that correlates translations with visions.

> 2 Corinthians 12:1-3
> ...I will come to visions and revelations of the Lord. **(2)**I knew a man in Christ above fourteen years ago, (whether in the body, I cannot tell; or whether out of the body, I cannot tell: God knoweth;) such an one caught up to the third heaven. **(3)**And I knew such a man, (whether in the body, or out of the body, I cannot tell: God knoweth;)

Translations both in-the-body and outer body experiences come under the classification of visions. This is why Paul in the previous text is speaking of a vision in which there is a vertical translation into heaven. This type of visitation is explained to be possible both in-the-body and out-of-the-body. When a vision is out-of-the-body we can still experience the same type of sensory capabilities and perceptions just as real as and even more real than we experience them in our own physical bodies.

I want to reiterate that in a vision it is possible to travel in the Spirit just like Ezekiel did in chapters three, eight, and multiple other chapters of his prophetic writings. It is therefore scriptural to conclude that Philip's translation in Acts 8:39-40 was also part of the fulfillment of Joel's prophecy concerning dreams and visions in the last days, which began to manifest in Acts 2:16-24.

It was in a vision that Ezekiel was carried away in the Spirit from among captives into the city of Jerusalem. He was also told to eat in a particular vision, and it was so real to him that the food became bitter to his stomach. Along with traveling, eating, and even the emotional sensations of weeping, Ezekiel also carried on conversations with the Lord and angelic messengers within the visions God had given to him. As you search the following charts you will find scriptural references of both horizontal and vertical translations and you will be able to locate the specific previously mentioned examples. However, prior to looking at the charts lets first look at another great example of an outer body translation.

Examples of Outer Body Translations:

Colossians 2:5
For though I be absent in the flesh, <u>yet am I with you in the spirit, joying and beholding your order,</u> and the stedfastness of your faith in Christ.

There's a connection in the presence of God between all believers. Now please do not get weird on me, or take this to the extreme, but I believe that it is possible that when Paul wanted to connect with the believers represented at Colossians 2:5, he would just get in the Spirit and the Lord would take him on a journey to their location. It is not doctrine, but it is certainly food for thought.

However, in the previous text when Paul said that he was present in spirit, he was not speaking metaphorically. He was literally translated in the Spirit to that location. The reality is that what is known as astral-projection among the occult world is scripturally known as translations, which normally takes place in visionary experiences. The Apostles and Prophets of old experienced this phenomenon long before the witches and warlocks. The following scripture is another great example.

Acts 16:9-10
And a vision appeared to Paul in the night; There stood a man of Macedonia, and prayed him, saying, Come over into Macedonia, and help us. **(10)**And after he had seen the vision, immediately we endeavoured to go into Macedonia, assuredly gathering that the Lord had called us for to preach the gospel unto them.

In Acts 16:9-10, Paul recognized that it was the Lord speaking to him through a man who had come to him from Macedonia in a vision. What happens when believers today began to communicate by means of translation just as Philip, Ezekiel, and the man from Macedonia did?[1] (Ezekiel 3:14-15; Acts 8:39-40) Though this is "RARE" it is very possible. The following charts more scriptural references of both horizontal and vertical translations.

Horizontal Translations:

Jesus
(Luke 24:31; John 6:19-21; John 20:26)

Elijah
(1 Kings 18:44-46 accelerated speed)

Ezekiel
(Ezekiel 3; 8; 11; 37; 40; 41; 44)

Philip
(Acts 8:39-40)

Paul
(Colossians 2:5)
(An outer body horizontal translation.)

Vertical Translations:

Jesus
(John 3:13; Acts 1:9, 10)

Elijah
(2 Kings 2:11)

Enoch
(Hebrews 11:5)

Paul
(2 Corinthians 12:1-4)

John
(Revelations 4:1-2)

Other Revelations:

1. Smells:

A Spirit of revelation can come upon the believer in a way that opens our sense of smell to the fragrance of the Lord in Worship as seen in Psalms 45:8. Earlier in the chapter we have expounded upon how the word taste in the Hebrew means to experience with all of the senses. Therefore, according to Psalms 34:8 not only can we taste, hear, and see that the Lord is good, but we can also smell and see that the Lord is good.

Although it seems kind of strange, I and countless others at times have discerned the presence of the Lord and also the presence of demons simply through the sense of smell. It is scientifically proven that there are countless nerve endings connected to our sense of smell alone. Just think of how our lives would be here in earth if we could not smell the fragrance of flowers, food, or the likes.

Likewise, I don't believe that God would allow the sense of smell to go to waste when it comes to experiencing Him in the Spirit realm. In fact, when the high priest would go into the Holy of Holies, the scriptures indicate that there were four fragrances that the priests were accustomed to in that place. We shouldn't forget that this very concept of fragrance and incense originated in the heavenly tabernacle that was shown to Moses on the mountain. God in His wisdom designed fragrance with an ability to create intended moods. Although it may seem insignificant, there is an incense that comes in the presence of the Lord and even an incense released to God in our praises and in our worship.

2. Prophetic Sounds:

    A. Acts 2:2 sound of wind
    B. Judges 7:20-22 sound of an army
    C. 2 Samuel 5:24 sound of the going

The previous are literal examples of the sound of heaven. However, prophetic sounds are normally administered through music in our day or time, yet only anointed musicians have the ability to play the sound they hear in the Spirit while others play to be heard. Nevertheless, prophetic sounds have great significance in the earth today.

A sound is a vibration and can be released to cause a shaking (1 Kings 1:40). Sounds are also scientifically proven to be light. When God releases a prophetic sound it can overthrow darkness in the earth. A great illustration of this is how the evil spirit would leave king Saul as David ministered the prophetic sound on the harp. I recommend readers to search out teaching on prophetic sounds by Ray Hughes.

3. The Audible Voice of God:

There are numerous examples of the audible voice of God in scripture. Below are only a limited few listed to show the consistency of this type of revelation in scripture throughout both the Old and New Testament.

    A. King Nebuchadnezzar

Daniel 4:31
While the word was in the king's mouth, there fell a voice from heaven, saying, O king Nebuchadnezzar, to thee it is spoken; The kingdom is departed from thee.

    B. The baptism of Jesus

Luke 3:22
And the Holy Ghost descended in a bodily shape like a dove upon him, and a voice came from heaven, which said, Thou art my beloved Son; in thee I am well pleased.

C. Gentiles

John 12:28-30
Father, glorify thy name. Then came there a voice from heaven, saying, I have both glorified it, and will glorify it again. **(29)** The people therefore, that stood by, and heard it, said that it thundered: others said, an angel spake to him. **(30)** Jesus answered and said, this voice came not because of me, but for your sakes.

D. Those traveling with Saul

Acts 9:7
And the men which journeyed with him stood speechless, hearing a voice, but seeing no man.

E. Peter on the roof top

Acts 10:15
And the voice spake unto him again the second time, what God hath cleansed, that call not thou common.

4. Dreams and Slumbering:

Job 33:14-15 (See also Job 33:14-30)
For God speaketh once, yea twice, yet man perceiveth it not. In a dream, in a vision of the night, when deep sleep falleth upon men, in slumberings upon the bed;

Dreams and Visions are the language of the Holy Ghost. They are significant in that our spirits don't sleep (Song of Solomon 5:2). While our physical bodies rest, deep continues to call out to deep and God continues to interact with our spirit man. Our dreams are not just our imagination. In fact, the very plan of our salvation was communicated through a dream.[1]

Furthermore, dreams are significant in the fact that Solomon received wisdom and wealth in a dream. He awoke from his sleep with an impartation for wealth and wisdom (1 Kings 3:11-15). Through prophetic revelation Solomon arose from a dream as the wisest man upon the earth. Dreams can also come as a prophetic administration in which a person dreams another person's dream and is given the interpretation of the dream in order to convey the word of the Lord to the original dreamer (Daniel 2:6, 19).

5. Trances:

In the Old Testament the word "trance" is italicized meaning that it is not used directly in the original writings (Numbers 24:4, 16). At times people would go into what was referred to as a "deep sleep", which in many occasions is equivalent to what a trance is in the New Testament. In every occurrence this type of "deep sleep" was not a result of time or tiredness but the result of an encounter with God (Job 33:15). In fact, the Hebrew word "tardemah" is used for a divinely induced heavy sleep. In other words, a trance is like God's amnesty before major operations.

The word trance in the Greek is actually defined as ecstasy or frozen shock. This means that in a trance, God completely apprehends not only our hearts and minds as in vision, but also our bodies so that there is complete focus and attention on the vision that He is showing us. Therefore, trances deal more with the state we're in while receiving a vision or revelation. It is while in that state, that it is as if everything in life is put on pause while nothing else matters but the unfolding and revealing of God's purposes and plans.

Other examples of Trances:
(Trances likened to deep sleep)

A. Adam

Genesis 2:21
And the LORD God caused a deep sleep to fall upon Adam, and he slept: and he took one of his ribs, and closed up the flesh instead thereof;

B. Abraham

Genesis 15:12
And when the sun was going down, a deep sleep fell upon Abram; and, lo, an horror of great darkness fell upon him.

C. Daniel

Daniel 8:17-18
So he came near where I stood: and when he came, I was afraid, and fell upon my face: but he said unto me, Understand, O son of man: for at the time of the end shall be the vision. (18) Now as he was speaking with me, I was in a deep sleep on my face toward the ground: but he touched me, and set me upright.[1] (See Daniel 10:7-9 & Acts 10:9-16; Acts 22:17)

In the New Testament "Trance" (1611) = Ecstasy; frozen shock

In a trance God completely apprehends our bodies and focus.

Conclusion:

With all of that information being released it would be a tragedy not to understand this next vital truth. The key to revelation is to seek the presence of the Lord Jesus and to avail ourselves to however He chooses to manifest Himself. There is safety when we are seeking Jesus and submitting ourselves to the study and obedience of His word along with accountability from local church leadership.

We should also understand that environments can be cultivated for revelation to flow (Hebrews 5:17). This means that if you are not experiencing revelation, you need to get in an atmosphere where people are. This doesn't mean that you have to leave the church you are currently attending, but it does mean that you must acclimate yourself to ministries that have already embraced what you are learning so far as normal and not far fetched.

Lastly, always remember that the flow of revelation does not always begin in blatant manifestations, yet our sensitivity can be developed to perceive the invisible world around us. So be encouraged even if you are not having angelic visitations and outer body experiences. Remember that its all about Jesus and if you get in His presence, He will blow your mind and have you in awe even if you never see an angel.

The reality is that many have already begun to penetrate supernatural realms and have simply not been aware of it. I believe for many this teaching has helped you acknowledge and celebrate the work of the Lord in your lives. For others there is a growth in hunger and insight.

Make no mistake about it, there is an invitation to experience God in the Supernatural and we shouldn't be afraid to entertain the Lord's presence in the ways mentioned in this chapter. I pray as you continue to seek the Lord and search out His word that you become more sensitive to the move of God in your life. And now that we understand various levels of prophetic revelation, in our next chapter we will take the time to understand their significance.

Chapter 4

Prophetic Acceleration:

The Relevance of Revelation

Key Points:
- Embrace why it is important in the life of every believer to understand and properly engage the supernatural
- Understand what prophetic acceleration is
- Understand the benefits of a God encounter
- Become opened minded concerning the things of the Spirit
- Avoid heart conditions that lead to blasphemy
- Distinguish the divine from the demonic: Prophetic movements vs. occult movements
- Understand the difference between prophecy & divination
- Understand the difference between signs & wonders and false signs & wonders

The Significance of Prophetic Revelation:

Why is it Important to Understand and Properly Engage the Supernatural?

There are two foundational things that we should establish prior to examining this chapter. One is that revelation should never deviate from the nature, heart, and mind of God as made known throughout scripture. We must remember that the objective of revelation is to know God and His nature as revealed in the bible. Therefore, the prophetic should never become a substitute for the word of God.

The second foundational thing that we should establish is that spiritual encounters do not make one person more spiritual than the next person. This is important to understand because there are many who use spiritual manipulation to control others through claims of divine authority given through spiritual experiences/prophetic encounters. I have noticed that there are many who follow such leaders while ignoring the principles of integrity and character that should be evident in the life of one who has truly encountered God.

I've also noticed that many have become prophetic fanatics at the expense of no longer trying the spirit to see if it is of God (1 John 4:1). This is why I have chosen not to include many of my personal encounters with God, but rather explain the supernatural from a scriptural context. Therefore, this chapter is designed to both validate the importance of revelatory experience and distinguish the authentic from the counterfeit.

As we embrace God's heart and mind concerning revelation we begin to understand that the supernatural does not manifest only to take us on a spiritual high, but it manifests for a purpose. Jesus made a powerful statement when He mentioned how wisdom is justified of her children (Luke 7:35). I believe that this principle should especially be applied to the supernatural in that we should expect fruit that both follows and remains after a genuine God encounter.

With that being understood, we should know that one of the primary reasons that God gives us prophetic revelation, in addition to revealing His nature to us, is so that He can establish things in the earth. Another reason is to accelerate the manifestation of His purposes. This is what I call prophetic acceleration, which is what takes place when God partners with man for the advancing of His kingdom.

God will often show us prophetically what He is doing behind the scenes, so that as we come into alignment with what is revealed, there is a grace to come into it's manifestation at an accelerated pace. Lets look at the next portion of this chapter to show us how.

Revelation is a Witness in the Earth: 1 John 5:7-12

Everything God does in the earth must be established by two to three witnesses or confirmations (Matthew 18:16), which are both words that can be used interchangeably. The supernatural is unique in that multiple witnesses (confirmations) can be administered within one revelatory/supernatural experience. In other words, the levels of revelation mentioned in the previous chapter are often clustered in the way they are experienced. This is why some supernatural encounters seem more dramatic than others.

For example, the initial impact of an impression may differ than that of a vision in that a vision could include not only impressions, but also visual components, along with travel into heavenly realms, and maybe even the audible voice of God. It is important for us to understand that the extremity of such a visionary encounter, as opposed to the impression alone, would do more than seize our attention to leave us in a state of awe. The magnitude of such a God encounter would not only shake us to the core of our being, but it would bear multiple witnesses in the earth and bring confirmation to our spirits concerning the purposes of God.

God has chosen not to do anything in the earth until after He first reveals what He is doing (Amos 3:7). Therefore, revelation can at times be a witness in the earth of what God is doing in the Spirit realm inviting us to cooperate in the fulfillment of its intended purpose. As we partner with God in the supernatural there is an ability to quickly establish things, which will otherwise take longer to establish apart from the wisdom of God. In other words, God can do more with us in one encounter with Himself, than we could do in a lifetime. A great example of this is the dream that Joseph interpreted for Pharaoh in Genesis 41.

Genesis 41:25, 32
(25)...the dream of Pharaoh is one: (32) And for that the dream was doubled unto Pharaoh twice; it is because the thing is established by God, and God will shortly bring it to pass.

There are key truths we must pay close attention to in the previous verses of Genesis 41. First of all, God was establishing something which according to Matthew 18:16 required two to three witnesses (confirmations). Secondly, we should understand that the supernatural (revelation) experience God chose to give Pharaoh was a dream.

Verse thirty-two of Genesis 41 says that the dream was "doubled twice," but in verse twenty-five Joseph said that the dream was "one." What does this mean? If we study the scriptures in context according to verses fifteen through twenty-five, Pharaoh had an encounter with the Lord as he slept, in which he dreamed two dreams.

This would actually be equivalent to having "one" dream, which played out "two" different scenes. This is why the scriptures say that the dream was one. God used a dream to give Pharaoh two confirmations in one night.

God gave Pharaoh "one" supernatural experience that contained two "witnesses" (confirmations) within itself. And according to Genesis 41:32, God allowed this revelation to be given to Pharaoh because he wanted to quickly bring the vision to pass. For this to happen, two witnesses were needed in order for the vision to come to pass and be established in the earth.

The dream had to be given in a way that brought the necessary confirmation for Joseph to properly interpret and have wisdom to give detailed instructions concerning how Egypt should cooperate with God during an impending recession in ways to suffer minimum economic lost. If this revelation had not been given a recession that was meant to last seven years could have been prolonged (Genesis 42:25-32). Therefore, it was because of this encounter with God that this nation was prophetically accelerated through a time of lack and drought.

Another great example of this is found in Jeremiah 1:12.

Jeremiah 1:12
Then said the Lord unto me, Thou hast well seen: for I will hasten my word to perform it.

If we look at the previous scripture in context of Jeremiah 1:11-12, we learn that it wasn't until Jeremiah both saw the vision and had heard the word of the Lord that God promised to quickly (hasten) perform His word. Why is this? It is because "the word" that Jeremiah heard represented the first "witness" (confirmation). The second "witness" was "the vision" that Jeremiah saw. The two "witnesses" were the criteria for God to establish that particular purpose in the Earth. Here again we see "multiple confirmations" (witnesses) being administered within "one revelatory experience."

The last example of this truth is found in the New Testament.

Acts 11:10-11
And this was done three times: and all were drawn up again into heaven. (11) And, behold, immediately there were three men already come unto the house where I was, sent from Caesarea unto me.

In order to get a full account of this story we must read Acts 10:9-48 and Acts 11:4-15. To make a long story short, Peter had "one experience" with God whereby he was taken into a trance in which "three times" an open vision was played before his eyes while hearing the audible voice of God. The revelatory experience carried "three witnesses" (confirmations) within itself, which means God was establishing this thing quickly.

If we look at the text closely we will find that one witness was established in the trance, another in the open vision, and the third and final in the audible voice of God. Not only were three revelatory experiences administered, but they were also rehearsed on three occasions. We notice that it was high priority on the Lord's agenda to get Peter's attention because, in this case, Peter needed revelation so that he could catch up with what God was doing. Let me explain.

God had already spoken to Cornelius through an Angel that he should send men to Joppa to find Peter. Three men were then sent to find Peter in order that the Gentiles could hear the gospel, but Peter had not yet been brought up to speed. It was only a matter of moments before the will of God would come knocking at his door in the form of three Gentiles. Therefore, the revelation was given to Peter in order for him to understand God's will for the Gentiles to hear the gospel.

Peter needed the revelation so that when gentiles arrived at his house he would not reject them. Therefore, God revealed to Peter supernaturally that He wanted him to communicate the gospel to the gentiles and by the time Peter came out of the trance state from which he received the revelation three men were already at his door waiting to escort him to preach the word. I don't know about you, but that sounds pretty accelerated to me.

In addition to God accelerating the establishment of His purpose, it is a known fact that many experiences of revelation often come in times of need for clarity, help, or comfort. For example, many testimonies of God encounters and angelic intervention are during times of near death experiences, the lost of loved ones, or seasons of intense pressure (2 Kings 6:16-17).

The supernatural can also manifest depending on the reassurance we would need during a future season of hardship (Acts 9:5-16). A great example of this is Jacob's experience of the open heaven at Bethel, where he saw the Lord and also saw angels who were ascending and descending going back and forth in and out of heaven (Genesis 28:11-17). It was after Jacob left what he described to be the "gate of heaven" that he went to work for Laban over the period of fourteen years in an oppressive work -labor environment (Genesis 29: 25).

Jacob needed the reassurance of what God promised in his supernatural encounter at Bethel during the fourteen years of what seemed like a setback. We likewise will never lack a need to embrace God in the supernatural. And for whatever reason God chooses that we encounter the supernatural, I am prophesying that such occurrences are about to greatly increase. So as you continue to read I want to be sure that you rid yourself of anything that will cause you to fear or resist the supernatural things that are going to begin to take place in your life.

Removing Neglect and Fear

There are many other reasons why the supernatural is important. We will cover one more reason further along into the chapter, but first we must understand why it is not healthy to fear or the neglect the things of the Spirit. We will also begin to understand and avoid the things that cause a person to oppose the things of the Spirit.

It is very important that this foundation is laid as we continue to progress because the carnal mind is hostile against God neither can it learn spiritual things (Romans 8:7; 1Corinthians 2:14). This means that if we are not humble and open in our approach to learning about the supernatural we could be found resisting the grace of God in this area.

Isaiah 8: 18-20
Behold, I and the children whom the LORD hath given me are for signs and for wonders in Israel from the LORD of

hosts, which dwelleth in mount Zion. (19) And when they shall say unto you, Seek unto them that have familiar spirits, and unto wizards that peep, and that mutter: should not a people seek unto their God? for the living to the dead? (20) To the law and to the testimony: if they speak not according to this word, it is because there is no light in them.

"Two Things that Happen when we Neglect the Supernatural"

The light of God does not abide in us (See Isaiah 8:20)

The world seeks after the occult rather than after God (See Isaiah 8:19)

The Conflict:

Luke 16:8
for the children of this world are in their generation wiser than the children of light.

When Jesus said that the children of the world are wiser in Luke 16:8, one of the things that He meant was that at times the people who are of the world are more ready to embrace the principles by which they function and live. In our day and time this statement still holds true especially when pertaining to spiritual things. God has given us a spiritual inheritance and He is waiting for us to embrace it, yet at times the world seems to be more willing to acknowledge things that are spiritual in nature. The demonic often offers the world a counterfeit supernatural, yet the things of the Spirit belong to the church and not to the occult. In the midst of growing deception, we must understand as believers that what Jesus has given the church, pertaining to the supernatural, is more powerful than what the occult offers the world.

Because of our neglect toward the supernatural many have become fearful, ignorant, critical, or deceived towards the things of God. Also, because of a lack of scriptural principles and standards concerning spiritual things, many have been seduced by familiar spirits to seek after witchcraft and the new age. Many have embraced the deceptions of the occult because they are yet to understand that what they seek after in the spiritual realm originates and is only complete in the Lord Jesus Christ.

One of the main roles of apostolic and prophetic ministry is to educate the church concerning the things of the Spirit (Ephesians 1:17-23; Ephesians 3:16-21; Colossians 1:9-14). We are living in a day in time in which believers must embrace the supernatural as never before and be able to discern what is and is not acceptable according to the scriptures. There is no scriptural New Testament Christianity that exists apart from the supernatural. And it will be very difficult if not impossible for the church to function effectively in this hour apart from walking in their spiritual inheritance. We must be willing to pay the price to walk in God's supernatural realm, which leads me to part two of this chapter.

Prophetic Acceleration Part Two:
Bearing the Stigma of the Supernatural:

Romans 3:3-4
For what if some did not believe? shall their unbelief make the faith of God without effect? **(4)**God forbid: yea, let God be true, but every man a liar; as it is written, That thou mightest be justified in thy sayings, and mightest overcome when thou art judged.

Now that we understand why it is important not to neglect the supernatural we must also understand that there is a price to pay as we embrace it. With all of the glories and wonders of God included, one walking in the Spirit has a cross to carry. This lifestyle is often highly persecuted and stigmatized with the risk of being misunderstood, envied, and even blasphemed.

Those who walk in the supernatural must understand that people who are not "spiritually minded" are forced to either accept the supernatural or directly oppose it. Sadly, many people make the wrong choices when it comes to spiritual matters. The reason being is simply ignorance.

History shows that when the secular accepts the supernatural it is recognized as nothing more than an impressive phenomenon and often sought out through the occult. Vice versa when the religious oppose the supernatural it is often accused of being associated with darkness and evil. Therefore, it is important that people in general are taught the supernatural from a scriptural perspective.

The lives of Jesus and Daniel are great examples of the way people respond to spiritual things when its culture does not understand the Spirit realm from the proper biblical foundation. The following scriptures show references of Jesus being accused of having a demon and also Daniel being nicknamed after a cultic order of that day.

Examples:

A) Daniel 4:7-8 a prophet named "Belteshazzar" after the occult

The name "Belteshazzar" means "spirit of the holy gods" which was a name derived from an occult belief in the Babylonian culture.

B) Luke 11:14-17 "Jesus accused of a demon"

Avoiding Blasphemy:

Isaiah 28:11-12
For the LORD shall rise up as in mount Perazim, he shall be wroth as in the valley of Gibeon, that he may do his work, his strange work; and bring to pass his act, his strange act. **(22)**Now therefore be ye not mockers, lest your bands be made strong: for I have heard from the Lord GOD of hosts a consumption, even determined upon the whole earth.

Isaiah 28:11 speaks of the strange works and strange acts of God. This simply means that God at times does things that can seem foreign to us. In times like these, we must be careful we don't follow the pattern of those who resist the supernatural.

Those who build memorials around the way that God moved in the past often oppose the way that God chooses to manifest Himself in the present. In order to avoid this we should begin to understand the difference between the "ways" and "acts" of God. His "ways" speak of His character and nature. His "acts" speak of the way (method) that He manifests both Himself and His power.

Although the "ways" of God remain the same, the "acts" of God may vary. Therefore, we must always receive the things of the Spirit with a humble mind and heart. We should be childlike, teachable, and quick to learn. If we have doubts concerning spiritual manifestations we should not dismiss them altogether immediately.

We should examine the manifestations we experience by the word of God, because it takes time and maturity in order to discern whether something is truly of God or not when it is initially introduced. Therefore, we should neither be quick to associate the supernatural with the demonic or quick to associate the unknown to the divine. We should rather try the spirit by the word of God in order to see if it is of God or not (1 John 4:1).

Heart Conditions that Lead to Blasphemy:

> 1 Timothy 1:13
> Who was before a blasphemer, and a persecutor, and injurious: but I obtained mercy, because I did it ignorantly in unbelief.

1 Timothy 1:13 is interesting in the fact that Paul not only acknowledges that he was formerly a blasphemer and persecutor, but also acknowledges the root cause of the problem. Paul acknowledges the conditions of his heart that led to blasphemy to be ignorance and unbelief. We can learn from this text and others that there are certain things in a person's heart that can cause a person to blaspheme the things of the Spirit. For instance, although the previous is very helpful insight, we should also understand that in addition ignorance and unbelief there are other heart conditions that can lead to blasphemy according to Luke 12:1-10.

In Luke 12 Jesus is warning His disciples concerning the blasphemy of the Holy Ghost. The warning was initiated after the Pharisees and chief priest had begun to speak against the things of the Spirit. The warning was also given in the context of Jesus exposing their hypocrisy. If we take a closer look at Luke 12:1-10, the religious leaders of the day, along with hypocrisy, were dealing with the fear of man, pride, and envy in their hearts. Ultimately any one of these things in our heart can cause us to eventually blaspheme or persecute the things of God, one way or the other. A great example of this is found in Acts 13:44-45.

> Acts 13:44-45
> And the next sabbath day came almost the whole city together to hear the word of God. **(45)** But when the Jews saw the multitudes, they were filled with envy, and spake against those things which were spoken by Paul, contradicting and blaspheming.

Acts 13:44-45 helps us understand the mental disposition of those who blaspheme the things of the Spirit of God. The religious leaders in the scripture were overly concerned about their religious status and reputation among those who followed in their particular walk of faith. Therefore, it was easy for them to teach the scriptures and simultaneously speak against Jesus, the early church, or the ministry of the Holy Spirit. Basically, if anything appeared to be more successful, or opposed to what they were accustomed to in the eyes of their followers, there was almost always an immediate resolve to envy it as well as an attempt to sabotage or destroy it.

The logic behind this type of behavior is quite simple. Pharisees and Sadducees always strive to be the most influential among their peers. In order to do so, they fight to protect their religious position or social status. Instead of truly having a heart to see Jesus glorified they disguise themselves in a "form of godliness" while pushing their own agenda.

Religious ideology is one of the main attacks against the power of God manifesting in a supernatural way. It will actually oppose the power of God in the name of doctrine (Mark 7:13). The only way to overcome this type of deception is to reach a place where we want to experience the Bible and not just know it. As believers we must continually develop a passion and desire to experience and know God in all of His fullness.

The Significance of Prophetic Revelation Continued:

As we conclude this chapter it is important to understand that when dealing with the supernatural, the prophetic and the ministry of signs and wonders go hand in hand. They are so important in the Kingdom of God that the enemy focuses much attention in perverting or polluting them. Throughout history God has always combined the prophetic and the ministry of signs and wonders to equip His people supernaturally, ultimately to impact this world for Jesus. There is no one that has ever done anything significant with God apart from the revelation of the Lord Jesus Christ. In like manner there is no one who has ever had a revelation of Jesus Christ who was not also empowered miraculously to help make Jesus known to others.

The demonstration of signs and wonders has a lot to do with revelation. A release of the supernatural through demonstration will often be preceded by an experience of the supernatural through revelation because of how the prophetic and the miraculous are inseparable. The enemy has worked overtime to either compromise or to pollute the true manifestation of the way man's heart is influenced by the supernatural.

In fact, there are so many compromised or either counterfeit illustrations of the prophetic and the miraculous that it is unwise not to distinguish the principles of their original God intended designs. Many through ignorance either attribute the Divine to being demonic or associate the demonic with the Divine. It is time that we begin to acquire adequate information whereby we can examine spiritual activity and discern whether they are of God (1 John 4:1).

Contrasting the Divine and the demonic:

"Prophecy vs. Divination"

Divination and the prophetic are operationally similar. The main difference between the two is rooted not in the way they function, but in the source from which they function. The source of divination is familiar spirits with an emphasis on idolatry and false religion while the source of the prophetic is the Holy Ghost with an emphasis on Jesus Christ. In order to properly distinguish the two, prophecy must be judged according to 1 Corinthians 14:29.

1 Corinthians 14:29
Let the prophets speak two or three, and let the other judge.

There is an amazing truth in 1 Corinthians 14:29 concerning judging prophecy that we must observe. As we do it will help us better discern whether prophecy or divination is in operation. The truth is that the true prophetic must undergo examination.

This involves the ability to hear God through the prophet rather than to depend on the prophet. Some people want a prophecy, but they don't want to hear or obey God. They want the supernatural, but they don't want the presence of Jesus.

Every experience of the supernatural that does not point back to the Lord Jesus is rooted in error. In like manner every prophecy that does not line up with the truth of scripture is not of God. It is only when we really have not submitted to the word of God that we open ourselves to the deception of divination.

2 Peter 1:19 teaches us that the "more sure word of prophecy" is in actuality the written word of God. We must be willing to seek God's voice through His word, which is the ultimate prophecy or we will open ourselves to divination which operates on the principle of idolatry according to Ezekiel 14:4. According to the following scripture, if we will not seek God, He will allow us to hear false prophetic messages based on the idolatry or vanity in our hearts.

> Ezekiel 14:4
> **(4)**...Every man of the house of Israel hat setteth up his idols in his heart, and putteth the stumblingblock of his iniquity before his face, and cometh to the prophet; I the Lord will answer him that cometh according to the multitude of his idols;

Another snare concerning divination is that it feeds upon the fear within the hearts of man. For example, King Saul did not become interested in divination until he became fearful of losing his kingdom. Likewise, so many people are deceived wanting to know the future.

Many are bound by the fear of failure. Others are paranoid about a so-called governmental conspiracy or the end of the world. The truth is that the future is about the redemption of Christ and the promises of God being fulfilled. The future is about the revelation of Jesus Christ and the New Covenant that has been given to us through His own blood.

Revelations 19:10 says that the testimony of Jesus is the spirit of prophecy. This means that true prophecy will always promote Jesus, hope, and repentance. Prophecy is an expression of the Lord's dominion over the events in time and the affairs of men. Even when prophecy comes to warn of impending danger there is always a redemptive plan of God in place.

Lastly, prophecies concerning the end times are primarily about the move of God and not the apocalypse. According to scripture the end of time does not represent the end of the world, but rather the beginning of the best. Therefore, even if there are negative predictions concerning the future there will always be a solution because prophecy will always glorify Jesus.

"Signs and Wonders vs. False Signs and Wonders"

Matthew 24:24
For there shall arise false Christs, and false prophets, and shall shew great signs and wonders; insomuch that, if it were possible, they shall deceive the very elect.

Often because of the way many misinterpret Matthew 24:24, anything associated with the supernatural has been labeled as deception by the ignorant or the unbelieving. It is obvious that we are yet to understand the supernatural particularly in a day in which we have warned against false signs and wonders to the extent that we are afraid of the manifestation of true signs and wonders. We must re-evaluate our approach to the miraculous. I believe we give the enemy more credit than he is due at times. Some read Matthew 24:24 and are so focused on the deception of false signs and wonders that they miss the truth that Jesus clearly declares that the elect will not be able to be deceived.

We must remember that false signs and wonders are not the only wonders taking place in the last days. According to Daniel 11 the people that know God will be strong and do exploits even in the midst of growing spiritual deception. In the last days there is an open confrontation and contrasting of the Divine and the demonic just as in the days of Elijah, Moses, and Daniel.

The Spirit of Elijah again cries out to the world and to the church to say "if God be God serve Him, but if baal be god serve him." How long will we hold between two opinions? The reality is that true power of God will either turn the heart of the hungry toward God, or harden the heart of the rebellious.

It is time that we remove the stigma from the supernatural and let the God who answers by fire be God. There is a need that we as believers begin to experience, demonstrate, and testify to the supernatural power of God. In a day in which the occults make false claim to deity and spirituality, it is only the true power of Jesus that can turn the heart of one who has been deceived.

The Finger of God
Luke 11:20; Exodus 8:19

Another thing to understand concerning the supernatural is that the demonstration of miracles, signs, wonders are at times referred to in scripture as the "finger of God". The finger of God speaks of the authenticity of God's power. The finger gives God's signature in a particular matter, which is heaven's royal seal or stamp of approval.

The scriptures teach that Jesus was approved of God by miracles, signs, and wonders in Acts 2:22. This is evidence of how God puts His signature on His people to distinguish them in the earth. A great example of this is when Moses asked for the presence of the Lord to go along with him and the children of Israel.

Moses understood that only the presence of the Lord could separate them from all other nations (Exodus 33:16). He also understood that as the presence of the Lord set Israel apart that the same presence of the Lord would also go before them and fight their battles. According to the scriptures it is the finger of God that both distinguishes the Divine and dismantles the demonic. The following scriptures are great examples of this truth.

Exodus 8:18-19
And the magicians did so with their enchantments to bring forth lice, but they could not: so there were lice upon man, and upon beast. **(19)** Then the magicians said unto Pharaoh, This is the finger of God: and Pharaoh's heart was hardened, and he hearkened not unto them; as the LORD had said.

Luke 11:20
But if I with the finger of God cast out devils, no doubt the kingdom of God is come upon you.

We are living in a day in which the powers behind idolatry, the new age, the occult, and the like will once again be confronted by those who walk in the supernatural power of Jesus Christ. I believe the power of God will once again bring warlocks, psychics, and idolaters to repentance.

In the days in which God activated Daniel in the supernatural, not only could the occult not duplicate the original, but they could no longer function in the counterfeit (Daniel 2:27; Daniel 4:7-8; Daniel 1:19-20).[1]

Those gone before us were signature in their day. They had the touch of God on their lives. The Old and New Testament patriarchs would overthrow demonic and religious strongholds all because the presence and power of God was manifested in a supernatural way. The following chart consists in New Testament examples of how walking in the supernatural empowered certain ones to confront and destroy the forces of darkness much like Moses, Daniel, and many others did in the Old Testament.

New Testament Examples of the Finger of God: Personal Study

"Dismantling the Demonic"

Mark 5:1-15 "Jesus and the demoniac"

Acts 8:9-13 "Peter and Simon the sorcerer"

Acts 13:6-12 "Elymas the sorcerer"

Acts 16:16-21 "Woman with the spirit of divination"

Acts 19:24-27 "the goddess Dianna"

In the very near future we will experience the supernatural through revelation of the prophetic in ways that equips us to release the supernatural through demonstration. As the church once again embraces the supernatural we will begin to experience the type of cultural reformation that is exemplified in the scriptures.

Reclaiming our spiritual heritage will be one of the keys it will take for the body of Christ to make the type of impact in this world for Jesus that was ordained in the beginning. And although it seems the church has regressed in fulfilling our original Kingdom mandate, I believe that God is prophetically accelerating us in this hour that we may reach our mission accomplished.

Chapter 5

The Angelic Kingdom

"But ye are come unto mount Zion, and unto the city of the living God, the heavenly Jerusalem, and to an innumerable company of angels," (Hebrews 12:22)

Key Points:
- Gain a healthy perspective and appreciation for the angelic kingdom
- Broaden your concept of heaven and angelic structures within heavenly places
- Understand the governmental structure of angels and their chain of command
- Understand different angels, how they look, and what they are assigned to do both in the heavens & in the earth
- Understand angelic activity & assistance in the life of the believer

Why Study the Angels

Comprehending the supernatural has a lot to do with understanding the principle of "As it is in heaven" (Matthew 6:10). Revelation not only gives us access to God, but also access to everything in the world in which he lives. Therefore, acquiring knowledge of the angelic kingdom will broaden our concept of heaven and will help us conceive spiritual realities.

Heaven is a Spirit world in which its very existence is comprised of Kingdoms. Our study on angels will bring clarity in understanding God's Spirit world called the heavens and also enlarge our paradigm concerning the Kingdom of God. It is almost impossible to completely explore the realms of revelations without expounding upon the angelic Kingdom because of the connection between the angelic guards and the prophetic mantle.

Jonathan Ferguson

A Basic Knowledge of Angels

There are over 300 biblical references of Angels. In them, the activity of angels is spoken of from the beginning to the end of time. Angels play a major role today concerning the eternal purposes of God. As we near the end of time there is an increase, not a decrease of their activity. In this chapter we will begin by covering some of the basic knowledge of angels and then progress into a greater perception of angels and the Spirit world in which they exist. Below is a chart that consists of basic things concerning angels that will help us gain a proper biblical perspective of their mere existence.

Angels have consciousness and free will (choices)	(Genesis 6:1-2, 4)
Angels can eat	(Psalm 78:25)
Angels have emotion & can be offended	(Exodus 23:20-21)
Angels are subject to Jesus	(1 Peter 3:21-22)
We judge angels not worship them	(Colossians 2:18; 1 Corinthians 6:3)
There are more angels than demons	(Hebrews 12:2; Matthew 26:53)

It is very interesting to note that angels are not mere robotic creatures. They are eternal beings created by God to serve Him and us as we will explain in more detail later. However, in addition to basic truths about the angels we should understand that they have been delegated great power by God to do what they have been created to do.

In fact, angels receive their authority and take on the attributes of God's strength in the presence of the Lord. Matthew 18:10 lets us know that the angels behold the face of the Father. This is significant in the fact that 2 Corinthians 3:17 informs us that anyone who beholds the face of God is transformed by the power of His presence. This means that in the presence of God it is almost impossible not to take on the attributes of His character and strength (Ezekiel 1:24). The story of the angel Gabriel in Luke 1:19 is a great example of this truth.

> Luke 1:19
> And the angel answering said unto him, <u>I am Gabriel, that stand in the presence of God</u>; and am sent to speak unto thee, and to shew thee these glad tidings.

It was the angel Gabriel's claim of standing in the presence of God whereby he used great authority in correcting Zacharias' unbelief concerning the pregnancy of Elizabeth (Luke 1:19-20). Gabriel signified that the basis of his authority in correcting Zacharias was that he stood in the presence of God. As a result of standing in God's presence, Gabriel had power from God to impress upon Zacharias the inability to physically speak for a season, which is a great example of how angels excel in the strength of the Lord (Psalm 103:20).

Psalm 103:20
Bless the LORD, ye his angels, that excel in strength, that do his commandments, hearkening unto the voice of his word.

How do Angels Look:

1 Corinthians 15:39-40
All flesh is not the same flesh: but there is one kind of flesh of men, another flesh of beasts, another of fishes, and another of birds. **(40)** There are also celestial bodies, and bodies terrestrial: but the glory of the celestial is one, and the glory of the terrestrial is another.

The key terms to pay attention to in 1 Corinthians 15:39-40 in reference to angels are "celestial" and "terrestrial" bodies. Angels are not flesh; they are ministering spirits although they have the ability to take on both terrestrial and celestial bodies. For example the scriptures make reference to both the man Gabriel and the angel Gabriel. When the scriptures reference the man Gabriel, it speaks of when Gabriel appears in the likeness of a man, which is his terrestrial body form (Hebrews 13:2). The angel Gabriel speaks of when Gabriel appears in the glory of his angelic form, which is celestial.

How is this possible? Though angels are ministering spirits, a spirit is yet a word and a word can become flesh and dwell among us (John 1:14; John 6:63). Therefore, 1 Corinthians 15:39-40 is simply speaking of the different glories of various bodily forms.

Basically, just like every form of creature that God created, angels have different forms and appearances. Though angels can appear in the likeness of human forms, they also have their own classifications of different bodily forms. In fact, angels are very diverse in their appearance according to scriptures. The following chart is designed to show us the different ways that angels can appear:

Diverse Angelic Appearances:

Likeness of men- Daniel 8:15
Men in linen and bright clothing- Revelations 15:6
Pure light and glory- Luke 2:9
Angels with wings- Isaiah 6:2
Angels without wings (unaware)- Hebrews 13:2
Chariots and horses of fire- 2 Kings 6:17
Unusual creatures and beasts- Revelations 4:6-8
Pillars of fire- Hebrews 1:7
Giant angelic beings- Revelations 10:1
Angels with the appearance of lightning- Daniel 10:6
Angels with coverings of precious stones and jewels- Ezekiel 28:13-14
Angels with coverings of metals and colors- Ezekiel 40:3

Understanding Angels in the Spirit World

Angels exist within every dimension of the Heavens. Let me explain. As we understand the Spirit world we discover that there are different dimensions of the heavens. We also see that there are dimensions of the heavens that are directly accessible from the earth.

Accessing heaven is not always about ascending upward. The bible says that God established the pillars of the earth and set the world upon it. This would have to mean that the earth and the world are two different things.

The earth is the literal land that we walk on. The world is the cosmos or systems that drive the progress of humanity. If the world is set upon the earth that means that there are spiritual realms and dimensions that are accessible within the earth's atmosphere.

These spiritual dimensions that are directly accessible in the earth's atmosphere are referred to according to Genesis 1:20 as the open firmament of the heavens. The open firmament is the last dimension of the heavens mentioned as being created in Genesis. There are three dimensions of the heavens mentioned in the creation account of Genesis that we expound upon in great detail in the next chapter entitled "Open Heavens." The three dimensions of the heavens mentioned in the creation account of Genesis have biblical references of angels stationary within all three dimensions.

Angels in the 3rd dimension of the Heavens
(See Revelations 4 & 5)

Angels in The 2nd
(See Colossians 1:16; Jude 6)

Angels in the 1st
(See Genesis 32:2)

God doesn't necessarily have to send us an angel from heaven but there are angels already assigned to us in the earth. Angelic activity is very common in the earth. Just because we don't see angels does not mean they are not here.

The Scriptures teach that it can be a normal thing to entertain angels unaware (Hebrews 13:2). Just as much as angelic encounters take place when God sends messengers from heaven they can also take place when we simply become more aware of the spirit world that exists around us. A great example of becoming aware of angelic activity is found in Genesis 28:12.

> Genesis 28:12
> ..and behold a ladder set up on the earth, and the top of it reached to heaven: and behold the angels of God ascending and descending on it.

Genesis chapter twenty-eight is unique in that there are angels ascending "first" and afterwards descending. This means that the angels were not coming from heaven into the earth, but they were going up first into the heavens from the earth. It was an open heaven access point. Whenever we come into the presence of the Lord there are portals that open to us so we access things in earth as they are in heaven. There are gates, doors, windows, and the like that give us access into heavenly revelation in which we will cover in the next chapter.

Jonathan Ferguson

Understanding Angelic Structure:

> Hebrews 1:7, 14
> ...who maketh His angels ministering spirits....(14) Are they not all ministering spirits...

The scriptures clearly state that "ALL" angels are ministering spirits. This means that the angels minister to God and on God's behalf. They also minister to us and on our behalf as we are in the presence of God.

There are many examples of this truth and a structure in which angels carry this out. We will have a greater understanding of angelic structures as we better understand the different categories that angels serve or minister in as mentioned in scripture. Let's start by understanding the angels that minister directly in the presence of the Lord.

Angels Ministering in His Presence:

The angels that serve in the presence of the Lord are different than the angels that are assigned to attend to us. In fact, the angels that minister in the presence of the Lord only have dealings with us as we are in that same presence in which they are ministering to the Lord.

1. Seraphs

> Isaiah 6:2-3, 6
> Above it stood the seraphims: each one had six wings; with twain he covered his face, and with twain he covered his feet, and with twain he did fly. **(3)**And one cried unto another, and said, Holy, holy, holy, is the LORD of hosts: the whole earth is full of his glory. **(6)**Then flew one of the seraphims unto me, having a live coal in his hand, which he had taken with the tongs from off the altar:

Seraphs attend directly to the presence and Glory of God. An interesting factor in the previous scripture is that these same angels ministering to the Lord began also to minister to Isaiah. Another great example of this is concerning the angels coming to Daniel as he was in prayer. Although the angels that Daniel encountered were not seraphs, they were in fact angels that were sent directly from the presence of the Lord as opposed to angels that were assigned to the earth.

2. Elders

> Revelations 4:10
> The four and twenty elders fall down before him that sat on the throne, and worship him that liveth for ever and ever, and cast their crowns before the throne, saying, (See Revelations 5:14)

Elders serve in heaven's determinate counsel. A great illustration of this determinate counsel is the random thoughts that may be represented at times of critical decisions. There are many factors that undergo examination when certain choices are presented that will alter the course of our lives. Likewise, this council of elders represents the wisdom of God in critical decision making while neither conflicting with or tampering the Lord's sovereignty or providence.

> Acts 2:23
> Him, being delivered by the determinate counsel and foreknowledge of God, ye have taken, and by wicked hands have crucified and slain:

3. Cherubs

> Ezekiel 10:20
> This is the living creature that I saw under the God of Israel by the river of Chebar; and I knew that they were the cherubims.

Cherubim guard, protect, cover, and function as chariot escorts for God's Glory and His throne. Cherubs come in pairs of twos and fours. They are like the Divine bodyguards for the sacred things of Heaven.

Study Examples on What Cherubs Do:

- ➢ God riding on the cherubs as chariot escorts
  (See Ezekiel 1 & 10; Isaiah 66:15; 2 Samuel 22:11)

- ➢ Cherubs covering the mercy seat
  (See Exodus 25:18-20)

- ➢ Cherubs guarding the way to the tree of life
  (See Genesis 3:24)

Other Names for Cherubs are:

(Study examples continued)

- ➢ The Four Living Creatures
  (See Ezekiel 1:6-11; Ezekiel 10:9-20)

- ➢ The Four Beasts
  (See Revelations 4:6-8)

Cherubs appear four different ways in scripture.

STUDY SCRIPTURE REFFERENCES of how Cherubs look:

Cherubs with 1 face and 2 wings-
(Exodus 25:18-20)

Cherubs with 4 faces and 4 wings-
(Ezekiel 1 & 10)

Cherubs with 2 faces-
(Ezekiel 41:18)

Cherubs with 1 face (each) and 6 wings-
(Revelations 4:6-8)

Chain of Command: Broadening our Concepts

Governmental Levels of Angels

Now that we understand the reality of angels in the spirit world and how they minister to the Lord we must also understand that angels also exist and function among a governmental structure according to Colossians 1:16.

Colossians 1:16
> For by him were all things created, that are in heaven, and that are in earth, visible and invisible, whether they be thrones, or dominions, or principalities, or powers: all things were created by him, and for him:

The previous scripture reference deals with a succession of authorities and rank in the realm of the Spirit. This succession of authority is descriptive of the governmental structure among the angelic kingdoms. Another interesting thing to note according to the scripture is that this governmental structure existed in Christ before the rebellion of Lucifer and fallen angels. This means that demonic principalities and powers had their origin among an angelic hierarchy.

We will better understand the angelic structure as we understand two things. First, the order of principalities and powers is not demonic in nature. Secondly, not all of the angelic rulers rebelled with Lucifer. The governmental levels of the angelic kingdom presently exist in both the demonic and the divine worlds. They consist of both angelic beings and angelic structure and are ordered as follows:

Prince/Arch

(Jude 9; Dan 10:13, 21)

Thrones

(Colossians 1:16; Revelations 20:4; Daniel 7:9)

Dominions

(Ephesians 1:20; Colossians 1:16)

Principalities

(Ephesians 3:10)

Powers

(Roman 8:38; Ephesians 1:20)

Rulers/ Authorities

(1 Corinthians 15:24; 1 Peter 3:22; Ephesians 6:12)

Hosts

(Luke 2:13; Psalm 148:2)

Note: Although the rulers mentioned in Ephesians chapter six are demonic, we must remember that if angelic rulers exist, than all of them did not rebel with Lucifer.

Important Truths in Colossians

Colossians 1:16
For by him were all things created, that are in heaven, and that are in earth, visible and invisible, whether they be thrones, or dominions, or principalities, or powers: all things were created by him, and for him:

Notice that there's a distinction between heaven and the invisible in Colossians 1:16. There are things in heaven that do not necessarily have to be invisible and there are things in the earth that do not necessarily have to be visible. If God opened our eyes to discern the spirit world around us we would see thrones, dominions, principalities, and powers.

The scripture is showing us a governing body in the Spirit world consisting of angelic beings and angelic structures. It is dealing with the spiritual protocol that governs territories and delegated authorities in the Spirit world. Lets briefly decipher what each represents.

Thrones represent positions of mastery and sovereign ruler ship from which law and judgment is administered. Dominions represent territories and various jurisdictions. Lastly, principalities represent jurisdictional headship and do not exist without princes and delegated governing powers or deputies. There are spiritual powers and authorities that govern the natural world from the invisible world.

Great examples of this can be found in the books of Ezekiel and Daniel. In fact, Ezekiel 9:1-4 articulates very clearly that there were six angels that had charge over a specific city referenced. Just as we have presidents, kings, and governors in the natural there are also angels that operate as royal delegates having territories and jurisdictions in which they govern from. In fact, Jude 6 informs us that in the heavens there are estates and habitation that were created for the angels to dwell in.

The word estate in Jude 6 is defined as land, territory, and abode. The word habitation is defined as abode and housing. This means that this angelic realm is literally civilized. This means that there would have to be multiple territories, communities, and divisions of this "innumerable" company of angels (Hebrews 12:22). Although we do not know the extent of this fact, we do know that the angelic world is very structured.

Harmony and Unity:

Now as we are beginning to grasp a concept of the angelic divisions by biblical examples we must also be mindful of the fact that all of the angelic divisions work in harmony. For example, in a college or university, no matter what the major area of study may be, there are some basic courses that everyone must take. I believe a similar principle applies to the order of angels.

Although there are many different divisions of angels, I believe God can use any type of angel to bring a message to His people or even protect them. For example, according to Revelations 4, the same cherubim that never cease in worship are also involved in administering the judgments of God in Revelations 13.[1] How is this possible if the cherub angels are "only" assigned to a division of worship? This is a great example of Angels operating beyond our limited concepts of their roles and divisions.

According to Jesus, in John 1:50-51, there is a constant ascending and descending that takes place among the angels. Angels are not stationed only in Heaven. They are constantly moving strategically and in order, according to their assignments. Angels are always traveling between dimensions working in a unity to accomplish God's will (Luke 11:17).

In conclusion of this thought, we should remember that there is a host of different angelic functions. As we have previously learned, there are angels that primarily minister to the Lord such as cherubs, seraphs, and the like. There is also a governmental structure of angels such as thrones, principalities, archangels, and the like.

Lastly, there are many other categories of angels that are assigned by God to primarily serve the purposes and plans of God pertaining to humanity. These angels can include descriptions such as holy ones, mighty ones, hosts and many more, which we will partially cover. These angels do more for us than bring us messages and protect us. We should always keep in mind that there are exhaustive levels of functions and divisions in which these angels undergo service on a daily basis.

Two Most Unknown Angelic Divisions:

Watchers

> Daniel 4:13, 17
> I saw in the visions of my head upon my bed, and, behold, a watcher and an holy one came down from heaven; **(17)** This matter is by the decree of the watchers, and the demand by the word of the holy ones: to the intent that the living may know that the most High ruleth in the kingdom of men, and giveth it to whomsoever he will, and setteth up over it the basest of men. (Daniel 7:9, 10)

Just as there are watchmen in the natural that serve the Lord in intercession and prayer, these angels are watchers in the Spirit. They have the power to establish and initiate things in the earth according to God's will as we pray. They can also empower with information, dream interpretations, and strategies that we need in order to fulfill our prayer assignments. They have a steadfast word in their mouths (Hebrews 2:2) as they work very closely with intercessory prayer warriors.

Scribe Angels/Angels with Scrolls

> Ezekiel 40:3
> And he brought me thither, and, behold, there was a man, whose appearance was like the appearance of brass, with a line of flax in his hand, and a measuring reed; and he stood in the gate.

Zechariah 2:1-2
I lifted up mine eyes again, and looked, and behold a man with a measuring line in his hand. **(2)** Then said I, Whither goest thou? And he said unto me, To measure Jerusalem, to see what is the breadth thereof, and what is the length thereof.

These are the angels that do the recording in the books of Heaven. They are the angels that take assessments concerning gained or lost ground, attitudes, actions, prayers, and even how we treat people (Hebrews 13:2). They do this by balancing between what is written in heaven and what is recorded from the earth of our actions, thoughts, and conversations. These angels monitor, measure, and assess matters to make sure that the things in the earth are in proper alignment with the things in Heaven.

Other Examples of Angelic Involvement:

Angels in Healing and Deliverance
(Psalm 107:20; John 5:4)

Angels in Prayer
(Revelations 8:1-6; 1 Corinthians 13:1; 14:2; Daniel 9:21)

Angels that Strengthen
(Matthew 4:11; 1 Kings 19:4, 5)

Angels that do battle
(Daniel 4:35; 2 Kings 6:17)

Angels that Interpret Revelations and Escort into Heavenly Encounters
(Daniel 8:16; Daniel 9:21; Ezekiel 40)

Angels that administer judgment
(Genesis 19:21-22; Revelations 15:1)

Angels and Elemental Powers:

The mighty-strong ones

Isaiah 28:2
> Behold, the Lord hath a mighty and strong one, which as a tempest of hail and a destroying storm, as a flood of mighty waters overflowing, shall cast down to the earth with the hand.

There are angels that have power with the elements.

Angels and the Elements:

Fire
(Revelations 14:18; 16:8)

Water
(Revelations 16:5)

Wind
(Zechariah 5:9; Revelations 7:1)

The Earth (land)
(Daniel 10:7; Revelations 16:16-18)

Food 4 thought:

Mark 4:38
And he was in the hinder part of the ship, asleep on a pillow: and they awake him, and say unto him, Master, carest thou not that we perish?

Mark 5:1-2
> And they came over unto the other side of the sea, into the country of the Gadarenes. **(2)**And when he was come out of the ship, immediately there met him out of the tombs a man with an unclean spirit,

Everyone quotes from Mark 4 concerning when Jesus spoke peace to the storm. Although this is amazing, I think it is equally interesting, in this case, that Jesus didn't just speak peace, but He rebuked the winds. I believe that the winds were rebuked when Jesus discerned that He was dealing with more than a storm.

I believe that it was no coincidence that it was after that the winds were rebuked that Jesus and His disciples arrived at shore to be met by a man possessed with demons. The scriptures indicate that the demons within the man at the tombs controlled this particular region with fear. In other words, these territorial spirits aware of Jesus' arrival.

I believe that the demonic powers of this particular country were trying to confront Jesus through the winds and the sea in order to hinder Him from bringing deliverance. It is possible that even principalities at times will tamper with the elements of the earth to cause storms, earthquakes, and other catastrophes. My point is that if angels can do this in their fallen state, how much more can the angels of God be released in order to reverse the demonic plots of natural disasters?

Angels on Assignment:

Another interesting to know is that angels are assigned both personally and corporately. Thousands of angels could be assisting any given person, church, or nation at any given time depending on the purpose, the need, or simply the willingness to acknowledge and partner with them (2 Kings 6:17). The following references are other great examples of this truth.

Every person has at least one angel

> Matthew 18:10
> Take heed that ye despise not one of these little ones; for I say unto you, That in heaven their angels do always behold the face of my Father which is in heaven.

Churches have angels

> Revelation 1:20
> ....The seven stars are the angels of the seven churches: and the seven candlesticks which thou sawest are the seven churches.

Cities and Nations have angels

> Daniel 10:20-21
> Then said he, Knowest thou wherefore I come unto thee? and now will I return to fight with the prince of Persia: and when I am gone forth, lo, the prince of Grecia shall come. **(21)** But I will shew thee that which is noted in the scripture of truth: and there is none that holdeth with me in these things, but Michael your prince.

The Word Activates Angels

Psalms 103: 20
> Bless the LORD, ye his <u>angels</u>, that excel in strength, that do his commandments, <u>hearkening unto the voice of his word</u>.

Angels act in the power of God's presence and word according to Psalm 103:20. The book of Galatians gives us great examples of how this takes place. Galatians 3:19 says in short that the promise made by God was ordained by angels.

The word "ordain" means to arrange, institute, appoint, and enforce. This means that every time God speaks a word, angels are assigned to carry the word, attend to it, establish it, and enforce it. God doesn't need angels to enforce His word, but He chooses that angels enforce His word.

Another interesting fact about angels is that Psalms 103:20 mentions that they excel in strength in accordance to the voice of God's word. This means that angels have varying strength levels that are in correlation to the activation of God's word. This is why God tells us to war with the prophecy.

We are co-laboring with the angels for the fulfillment of the word. In fact, there are principalities and powers that are awaiting us to make known to them the manifold wisdom of God (Ephesians 3:10). If we are not doing our part we are not giving the angels anything to work with. Angels are strengthened in praise and in the decreeing of God's word.

The scripture says that the angels hearken to the voice of God's word. This is a very powerful truth that we must examine and understand. The voice of God and the voice of His word are two different things. The Voice of God is when God speaks. The voice of His word is like the sound of an echo released when we say what God has already said.

The angels move at the word of God in our mouths. Some argue whether we command angels or not. There is nowhere in scripture where men directly commanded angels, however the angels do respond to the believer that speaks the word of God. Angels respond to the voice of God's word as if God is speaking.

God's Voice = When God speaks

Voice of His Word = His word in our mouths
(Psalm 103:20)

Hebrews 1:7, 14
And of the angels he saith, Who maketh his angels spirits, and his ministers a flame of fire. **(14)** Are they not all ministering spirits, sent forth to minister for them who shall be heirs of salvation?

The scripture says clearly that the angels are assigned to minister to us. The word minister means to serve. As long as we are in the presence of the Lord and speaking the word the angels serve us.

A great example is when strength came on the angels as Daniel prayed in Daniel 10:12 and Daniel 9:21(See also Revelations 8: 1-6). Daniel's prayer life produced a strength that caused angels to be able to fly swiftly and break through demonic resistance. Another great example of how angels serve us is found in the scripture referenced below.

> Revelations 12:11
> And they overcame him by the blood of the lamb, and by the word of their testimony; and they loved not their lives unto the death.

Although Revelations 12:11 is a frequently quoted verse, many overlook a key element of its truth. The scripture says, "they overcame". If we look at this scripture in context according to Revelations 12:7-11 we better understand the portion of the text "they overcame". We discover that those who overcome are in reference to the angels as well as the believers.

More precisely, the "they" who "overcame," is in reference to the angels who were prevailing in spiritual battle through the word of the believer's "testimony". As the believers persisted in their faith concerning the blood of Jesus, and not loving their lives even unto death, God's angels were overcoming the devil and his angels through the spoken word of the believer's testimony (Revelations 12:7-11). Another way to see how this works in greater detail is to understand the power of binding and loosing according to Matthew 16:19.

> Matthew 16:19
> And I will give unto thee the keys of the kingdom of heaven: and whatsoever thou shalt bind on earth shall be bound in heaven: and whatsoever thou shalt loose on earth shall be loosed in heaven.

Binding and loosing in biblical times were legality terms. They speak of the judicial process of both confining and releasing a criminal in and out of prison. In the realm of the Spirit, this is accomplished by words spoken from our mouths. This is why the scripture says in Job 22:28 that we should decree a thing.

The word decree is another legality term dealing specifically with the authority we have in our words. The original writings of Jesus in Matthew 16:19 instruct us to bind and loose in the earth, what has already been bound and loosed in heaven. This means that if we speak in the earth based on what has been mandated in heaven, in turn Heaven will back us up in the earth.

God will respond and the angels will work on our behalf and in our favor. Our words establish the laws of heaven in the earth and then the angels reinforce these laws. As long as we are speaking the words of God, the angels move swiftly to assist us.

There are countless angles working to ensure our protection. They are ready to bring us miracles of healing, deliverance, and even financial increase. The angels are also sent at times to bring us interpretation of God's secrets and they are here to help us understand visions and dreams.

They have been sent by God to help fight our battles. They are always ready to serve, but they will not move until we prophesy. They will only interact with us as we interact with God and speak His word. According to 1 Peter 1:10-12 wherever the prophetic is in activation, revelation is flowing, Jesus is being glorified, the gospel is being preached, or the Holy Ghost is present; angels are very present and active.

1 Peter 1:10-12 teaches that the angels desire to look into and long to be apart of such matters. They understand their role in the partnership with humanity for God's purposes in the earth and it is their pleasure to serve us as we fulfill the will of God in the earth.

Chapter 6

Open Heavens

"....Surely the Lord is in this place; and I knew it not. And he was afraid, and said, how dreadful is this place! This is none other but the house of God, and this is the gate of heaven." (Genesis 28:16-17)

Key Points:
- Understand what an open heaven is: Get an open heaven concept
- Study the realms of heaven (1st, 2nd, 3rd heavens)
- Learn how to know when the heavens are closed
- Understand what happens when the heavens are opened
- Understand how to open the heavens
- Understand heaven as a literal place
- Understand relationship and correlation between the kingdom of God and open heavens

What is an Open Heaven?

Matthew 6:10
Thy kingdom come. Thy will be done in earth, as it is in heaven.

In Matthew 6:10, Jesus instructed us to pray that His Kingdom and His will would come into the earth as it is in heaven. This statement should automatically give us the awareness of two things. One, things are not in the earth as they are in heaven. Two, its God's desire and agenda that things come in earth as they are in heaven.

If we do not understand that God wants things in the earth as they are in heaven we will miss the impact that God originally designed heaven to have in our present lives. Some may not grasp the previous concept if in fact they only want to go to heaven in order to escape hell.

Yet, those who truly understand the kingdom of God understand that heaven is not merely an after life experience.

Although we do await a new heaven and a new earth, eternity begins now for the believer who is just as excited about bringing heaven into the earth as they are about transitioning to heaven eternally. I pray that the remainder of this chapter will stir a hunger in you not only to make it into heaven one day, but also to rather live under an open heaven now.

We are living in a period of time in which the things in heaven and earth are connecting, gathering, and being almost magnetically pulled together within Jesus Christ (Ephesians 1:10). In other words, an open heaven is simply when our world and God's world collide. It is when heaven invades the earth in Kingdom, in power, and in glory (Matthew 6:10-13).

As believers we know and understand that the earth is the Lord's and the fullness of it, yet we are not always aware of how intricately involved God is in the everyday affairs of man. One of the things that an open heaven represents is the awareness that comes to us of God's activity in the Spirit realm pertaining to our lives here in the earth. God is always moving for us in the Spirit, but we do not benefit from it unless we first acknowledge and cooperate with how He is moving.

We can only accomplish this, as there is a conscious awareness of the Lord's presence. This is why Isaiah prayed for the heavens to open and God to come down (Isaiah 64:1). It is as the heavens open that the presence of the Lord becomes tangible and Isaiah wanted to continue to be sensitive to and cooperate with what God was doing prophetically in the earth.

It was as the heavens opened that the Holy Spirit descended upon Jesus and led Him into His Kingdom assignment (Matthew 3:16). It was as the heavens opened that Ezekiel entered into the visions of God and began to prophesy. Also, according to Deuteronomy 28:12 it is the same opening of the heavens that causes the works of our hands to be blessed and successful. We are most productive in life when what's happening in the earth is in harmony with what's happening in the heavens.

The heavens must open causing an alignment of both worlds so that we are able to discern, acknowledge, and cooperate with the Kingdom and will of God in the earth.

Portals of Heaven

When people speak of open heavens they often speak of portals as well. As we have learned, there is a magnetic pull into the earth of things that have already been prepared for us in the heavens (Ephesians 1:10). The portals of heaven rather deal with the capacity in which things gravitate and manifest into the natural from the spiritual.

It is wise to scripturally validate what portals represent because of how they have become often mentioned in prophetic teachings throughout the body of Christ. The only scripture that can directly and biblically validate what portals represent foundationally is Mark 13:34 in which Jesus speaks of the "porter". The revelation of the portal is in the revelation of the porter.

Historically a portal was any gate, door, or etc. that a porter is assigned to watch. Therefore, the word portal is simply a word used in times past to describe an entryway. In fact, in the Old Testament, the word door and gate is often defined as a portal, which is why now the word has been adopted in our present church culture to have prophetic significance.

Therefore scriptural references of doors, gates, and windows could be prophetically symbolic of portals. They are prophetic pathways by which we enter within the heavenly realms. They are also channels by which the things of heaven enter into the earth.

Portals can be extended and opened over nations, families, local churches, cities, regions, and even individuals. In fact, these access points called portals can be seen throughout scripture within contexts that pertain to open heaven realities. For example, when the heavens opened in Mathew 3:16, Jesus was the portal, or in other words the access point for the heavens to open (see also John 1:50-51).

In Malachi 3:10, the scripture says that God will open a window as a portal access point for the blessing to be released because of our tithes and offerings. When the heavens opened for John while writing the book of revelations, a door was opened as a portal in which John was caught up and began to write the things that he had seen (Revelations 4:1). The pool of Bethesda in John chapter five even existed as a portal through which divine healing could flow.

Lastly, in Genesis 28:16-17, when Jacob became aware of the presence of the Lord he noticed that a gate had been opened as a portal. He not only noticed a gate but also a stairway in which angels were traveling back and forth in and out of heaven (Genesis 28:12). It is possible that these portals were stationed over the whole region of Bethel causing Bethel to be a place of heightened spiritual activity. When these portals open to the believer in the supernatural it is God's will that we pull from this reality in a way to transform, bless, and empower our lives.

There are heavenly places, spheres, and dimensions that we can access as these portals open up to us within the earth causing us to become direct recipients of God's kingdom benefits. The blessings, favor, and promises of the Lord become very evident in our lives. The make-up of heaven begins to infiltrate the earth as angels are assigned to our assistance and there is an intensity of revelation released. Every person that names the name of Jesus and is led by the Spirit of God has been granted access to live under an Open heaven.

Foundation: First, Second, and Third Heavens

Biblical concepts of heaven are distinctly different than what is religiously or traditionally understood. The word "heaven" is often plural in scripture. In fact, in the beginning God created "the heavens" not just heaven according to the original Hebraic translation.

There are three dimensions of the heavens mentioned in the biblical account of creation. We will explore this more in part two of this chapter. For now we will only establish a basic understanding concerning the three heavens in order to lay a foundation for expounding upon the open heaven concept.

Paul spoke of being "caught up" into the third heaven, which is the place where paradise is. It is the immediate abode of God and the place where His throne is established. It is the existence of the third heaven that implies the existence of second and first heavens, which correlates directly with the Genesis account of the heavens' creation.

In Genesis chapter one, the heavens were mentioned as being created in three different contexts. The first time the heavens were mention in creation it was in reference to the third heaven (Genesis 1:1). The next time the heavens were mentioned in creation they are in reference to the heaven's expanse among the galaxies (Genesis 1:8), which is what we call the second heavens. The last time the heavens were mentioned in creation it is in reference to the "open firmament" which is what we call the first heaven (Genesis 1:20).

It is the first heaven that consists of a spirit realm that literally exists in the skies above us and infiltrates the very air around us. I believe this represents how the earth is designed to open itself to the things of the Spirit. When this takes place spiritual atmospheres are created causing the realities of heaven to dwell among us behind the scenes, invisible to the naked eye.

As we understand this truth we will likewise begin to understand how much of heaven we can access while in the earth. The bible teaches more about heaven than being a place we go to if we're saved and as believers we should be interested in the entirety of what our heavenly citizenship includes. As we observe the scriptural references concerning open heavens in the following chart, we can better define what it consists of.

Open Heaven Blessings:

Open Heaven = The Blessing
(Deuteronomy 28:12)

Open Heaven = Visions and Revelations
(Ezekiel 1:1)

Open Heaven = Angelic Activity
(John 1:50-51)

Open Heaven = Abiding Presence of the Holy Spirit
(Matthew 3:16)

In addition to the previous references, the Garden of Eden is a great illustration of an open heaven. The word Eden is defined as "a place in God". Although there is more than one definition of the word Eden, the definition "a place in God" is more relevant in our study of open heavens.

As long as Adam and Eve were in Eden they were in a place in God. In fact, many theologians believe that the Garden of Eden was literally in heaven because they don't understand the concept of an open heaven. They don't understand how Adam and Eve were in earth and in a heavenly realm at the same time while in the garden. Truth is, as long as Adam and Eve were in Eden they had access to the heavens even while in the earth.

In fact, Genesis 2:8 teaches that the Lord planted the garden. It is safe to assume that in order for something to be planted it must be a seed, which is the beginning of a harvest. Therefore, if the garden was a seed that God planted in Eden, it means that the open heaven in Eden was the beginning of what God wanted in all the earth.

God took something that was perfect, planted it in the earth, placed man in the middle of it, and blessed him to expand its domain. Therefore, Adam's blessing and dominion in the earth was directly connected to the sphere in which God had placed him. God designed that we are blessed in the earth from the heavenly realm and has given us dominion to initiate the agendas of heaven in the earth. This is why things do not go well for us if we are not in tune with the Spirit of God.

I believe that this concept of life under an open heaven is how God originally designed life to be experienced in the earth from the time that God placed man in the garden. Many may disagree, yet despite the controversy, it is without doubt the life that is available to the believer through Christ Jesus (Ephesians 1:3/Ephesians 2:6). The optimum life requires experience of both heaven and earth.

This is most likely why after the end of this age scriptures teach that there will not only be a new heaven, but there will also be a new earth. Jesus is not coming back for us merely to grant us access into heaven. Although heaven is wonderful, God in His wisdom has decided that there will be heaven on earth. There will still be a heaven that is clearly distinct from the earth, but there will also be heaven on earth. Good news is, we don't have to wait until later, but we been granted to have a glimpse of this now through the power of the Holy Ghost inside of us (Luke 17:21; Romans 14:17).

The Concept: Understanding Open Heaven by Understanding Kingdom

> Matthew 6:33
> But seek ye first the kingdom of God, and his righteousness; and all these things shall be added unto you.
>
> John 18:36
> Jesus answered, My kingdom is not of this world:

Kingdom has become a very popular term in the Christian vocabulary. There are many things the Kingdom of God represents though many use the terminology loosely or meaninglessly. Many seek to understand the principles of God's Kingdom without fully embracing the reality of its existence.

Jesus clearly stated that the Kingdom of God is not of this world. The kingdom is the reality of another world manifesting itself in the earth. In fact, this other world is literally the Spirit world.

God has structured the Spirit world like a Kingdom and called it the heavens. A person who is seeking the Kingdom of God is automatically seeking the reality of an open heaven. Jesus was literally teaching us the benefits of seeking Him in the supernatural in Matthew 6:33 when He told us that if we sought the kingdom first that all the other good things in life would be added afterwards.

If we focus on seeking the blessing and the material things it will be left up to chance what we receive. The natural world guarantees no one anything in life, but if we seek the Kingdom, we will get an open heaven and receive all the blessings that come with it. Not only will we receive the blessings, but they will be commanded upon our lives and they will be pursuing us instead of us pursuing them (Deuteronomy 28:2, 12).

The primary message that Jesus preached was, "the Kingdom of heaven is at hand". And the phrase "at hand" is literally defined as "near always". Jesus also taught that the Kingdom of heaven is within us (Luke 17:21). This means that the heavens do not exist merely as a place located beyond the clouds. In addition to the heavens being above the clouds, the heavens are also "near" and "within".

Simply put, the kingdom of God is the reality of an open heaven, which is when things come in the earth the way they are in heaven (Matthew 6:10). Although we are in this world we are not of this world. We are connected to a world of greater reality that is intended to directly influence, invade, and bless our lives. We are not waiting on the day when we finally see the "pearly gates" of heaven. We are citizens of heaven now, and there are some blessings that God has intended to release in our lives now, supernaturally through an open heaven.

Contending for an Open Heaven: Heaven on Earth

In Matthew 11:12 the scripture says that the kingdom of God suffereth violence but the violent take it by force. The phrase "suffereth violence" comes from the same original word and means to forcefully advance. The meaning of this text is not that the Kingdom of God is under attack or being victimized, but is rather that the kingdom is forcefully advancing in the earth.

The move of God's kingdom is not passive therefore we must be aggressive in pursuing our Mathew 6:10 mandate of seeing things manifest in the earth as they are in heaven. The very spirit of Matthew 11:12 is a great example of what it means to contend for an open heaven. We can't afford to conform to life as normal. There must be a passion in us to experience the fullness of what God has for us.

The tragedy is that many are quicker to accept the reality of "what is" than they are to embrace and press into the reality of the Kingdom. God set before Israel both life and death and afterwards left it up to them to choose between the two opposite realities. Likewise, if we want to experience the blessings of an open heaven we must choose to contend for it. It is only as we will stir ourselves to relentlessly seek the Lord that we can see the heavens torn open over our lives (Isaiah 64:1, 7).

There are multiple scriptural references that show us how when the heavens are not open the earth does not produce the way it should (Luke 4:5; 2 Chronicles 7:13-14). For example, Deuteronomy 28:12, 23 informs us of specific blessings and curses that come into our lives as a result of either obedience or disobedience. Many have been yet to realize that these blessings and curses are not only a result of obedience and disobedience, but they are also a result of the heavens being either open or closed.

When we look at this particular text in Deuteronomy in full context, we see clearly that when the heavens are open the earth is blessed, but when the heavens are closed the earth is cursed (Deuteronomy 28:12, 23). One of the definitions for the word "cursed" is to devalue. This means that we will not reach our full potential in the earth when heaven is not involved.

After man reaches the end of all of his scientific theories, medical breakthroughs, inventions, and accomplishments there will always be one thing left missing. It is man's willingness to connect with God in the Spirit realm that is the missing link between science and technology. God only advances us in the natural as we connect with Him in the Spirit. He puts His "super" on our "natural" and afterwards life becomes full of possibilities.

As we press in to God by faith even the darkest and most negative things in our lives can be turned in our favor. In fact, most of the disappointment we experience and accept as normal in life is result of a closed heaven. This is not to imply that living under an open heaven is exclusive of hardship. An open heaven does not make us exempt of problems in life, but it does give us an alternative.

It gives us an opportunity to witness God take our lives and cause everything about them to work together towards our ultimate advantage. Heaven will open if we would contend for what God has promised. As we seek the Lord with our whole hearts and prioritize the things of the kingdom, heaven will invade our lives and we will touch God in ways that transform our lives forever (See Colossians 3:1-3). The heavens will open over our lives and advance us from the place where we are, into the place where we are destined to be in Jesus name.

Opens Heavens Part Two:

Heaven is the Real World

> Hebrews 8:5
> Who serve unto the example and <u>shadow of heavenly things</u>, as Moses was admonished of God when he was about to make the tabernacle: for, See, saith he, that thou <u>make all things according to the pattern shewed to thee in the mount</u>.

"Of heavenly things" in Hebrews 8:5 = that which is of true existence and reality

It is very interesting to note that in Hebrews 8:5, the phrase "of heavenly things" in the original language literally means "of true existence". This means that the things of heaven are those that are of true existence and reality. If we are going to truly embrace a scriptural understanding of heaven we must begin by understanding that heaven's state of existence is far more superior to that of the earth.

In fact, the heavens are the real world. In actuality, Spirit is the highest form of matter therefore; the spirit world is more real than the natural world. According to the scripture, in heaven we have a better and more enduring substance (Hew 10:34; 2 Corinthians 4:18).[1] How is this possible?

Everything Originates in the Spirit

> Hebrews 11:3
> ... things which are seen were not made of things which do appear.

The previous text teaches that the things we see are made of things that we do not see. This means that natural things are like mirror images of spiritual realities. You see, the earth was originally decorated to reflect the heavens. Every design in the natural has a spiritual blueprint (Hebrews 8:5; Acts 7:44).[1]

Everything we see in the natural was patterned after something that existed first in the Spirit because there is nothing new under the sun (Ecclesiastes 1:9). This means that there is nothing that exists in the earth that did not first exist in the heavens. For example, Jesus had always existed in the eternal, but He was not manifested in flesh until the appointed time (1 Peter 1:20).

These truths are important to understand in that the more we understand the heavens the more we will understand open heavens. When we mention heaven we're normally speaking in reference to what the scriptures refer to as the "heavens above the heavens" or the third heavens (2 Corinthians 12:2-4).). It is where paradise along with many other heavenly places exists.

This (third) dimension of the heavens is a very real, tangible, and inhabitable place. When the scriptures mention the better substance in heaven, the word substance literally means property, goods, and possessions (Hebrews 10:34). Heaven is not a mystical state of mind, neither is it just a peaceful after life experience.

When the scriptures say that God created the heavens, the word created literally means to sculpt and design. Scripture also refers to God as an architect and master builder (Hebrews 11:10). Heaven is full of things that serve as the prototype of things we experience in the earth. In fact, everything in the earth that is of any worth or value came from heaven (See James 1:17; Ecclesiastes 1:9).[1] The following chart consists of a list of things in the earth that originated in heaven.

Mountains

(Revelations 21:10)

Rivers

(Revelations 22:1)

Trees

(Revelations 22:2)

Mansions

(John 14:2)

Animals

(Revelations 6:2, 4, 8)

Streets

(Revelations 21:21)

Gates & Walls

(Revelations 21:10-11)

Food

(Luke 22:30; Psalm 78:23)

Cities & Geographical Locations

(Hebrews 11:10; Hebrews 12:22)

Cities & Geographical Locations:

We should understand that the third heaven is incredibly vast. In fact, within each dimension of the three heavens there are realms that the scriptures refer to as heavenly places. The scriptures also refer to these realms as, "the heavens of the heavens".

The "heavens ABOVE the heavens" are different than the "heavens OF the heavens". The "heavens ABOVE the heavens" simply illustrates how the heavens climb in heights. For instance, the first, second, and third heavens are examples of the "heavens ABOVE the heavens".

The "heavens OF the heavens" rather speak of how there are heavens within the heavens. In other words there are multiple heavenly places existing within each height of the heavens. There are heavenly places in the first heaven and there are heavenly places in the second and third heavens.

A good illustration of this is three different houses located on three different sides of a city. The houses are representative of the heavens. Each house exists in three different locations, which are representative of three different dimensions, and they each contain multiple rooms, which are representative of multiple heavenly places or realms.

The houses are heavens, the rooms are heavens, and all together they are the "heavens of the heavens". Just as there are multiple rooms in all three houses, there are also multiple heavenly places within the first, second, and third heavens.

The scriptures teach that God literally stretched the heavens. This means that the third heaven encompasses more than just a big room in which we sing worship songs for all eternity. Heaven is a lot more creative and interesting than what it is normally projected to be.

A great example of this is the heavenly city mentioned in the previous scriptural references. The city mentioned is only one of eight literal places or geographical locations in heaven mentioned in scripture. In fact, the scriptures also speak of a heavenly country (Hebrews 11:14-16). In order to be a country it would have to consist of multiple cities, states, and regions.

All of the concepts of livelihood, culture, and civilization originated in the third heavens. In fact, the culture of the third heavens is far more advanced than that of the earth. The third heaven is not a place in which we merely float in bright lights and on fluffy clouds for all eternity.

If we could imagine the earth in all of its beauty and in its original state before sin entered, then we would only be beginning to grasp the splendor and wonder of heaven. The following chart consists of seven additional references of geographical locations in heaven that will help us embrace heaven's creative make-up.

Seven Other Places in Heaven:

Paradise

(2Corinthians 12:2-4; Revelations 2:7)

The Throne Room/ Council Room

(Revelations 4 & 5)

The Holy Mountain

(Psalm 87; Psalm 15:1)

The True Heavenly Sanctuary

(Hebrews 8:2, 5-6; Acts 7:44)

The Storehouses

(Deuteronomy 28:12; Psalm 33:6-7)

The Father's House/ Many Mansions

(John 14:2)

The Banquet Houses, Rooms, and Tables

(Songs of Solomon 2:4; Luke 22:30)

God Rules the Second Heavens:

Ephesians 6:12
For we wrestle not against flesh and blood, but against principalities, against powers, against the rulers of the darkness of this world, against spiritual wickedness in high places.

Ephesians 1:20-21
Which he wrought in Christ, when he raised him from the dead, and set him at his own right hand in the heavenly places, **(21)**Far above all principality, and power, and might, and dominion, and every name that is named, not only in this world, but also in that which is to come:

Colossians 1:16
For <u>by him were all things created</u>, that are <u>in heaven</u>, and that are in earth, <u>visible and invisible</u>, whether they be thrones, or dominions, or principalities, or powers: all things were created by him, and for him:

When people think of the second heavens, it is normally in reference to demonic activity. Although this is true, we will never have a proper concept of the second heavens until we understand that God is ultimately the authority in that dimension. According to scripture, demonic principalities are clearly in a lower dimension of the heavens in which they do not have sovereign rule.

If we compare the text in Ephesians chapter six with the text in Ephesians chapter one, we can observe an amazing truth. In Ephesians 1:20-21 Jesus is seated in heavenly places. Likewise, in Ephesians 6:12 principalities and powers operate in heavenly places as well. They both exist in heavenly places, yet the dimension of the heavenly places in which they exist are different.

The heavenly place in which Christ is seated are in a higher dimension than the heavenly places from which the demonic principalities operate. Also according to the full context of Ephesians chapter one, the second heavens, where principalities abide, presently exists as the footstool of Christ. This is significant in that the feet represent the enforcing of God's law.

This is why God told Eve that the heel of her "foot" would crush the serpent. In Romans 16:20 He promises to crush satan under out feet and in Luke 10:17 we have power to tread over all the power of the enemy. Although warfare does take place in the second heavens it is important the believer begins to reclaim proper mindset of the authority God has given to assist the believer in this realm against demonic warfare.

The placement that Jesus has in the heavenlies above principalities and powers is descriptive of His complete dominion in both the third and second heavens. In fact, the principalities of the second heavens were originally created in Christ Jesus according to Colossians 1:16. It was not until after the fall of the former archangel, Lucifer, that demonic forces began seeking to establish authority in this dimension.

We must also remember that not all of the angelic authorities of Colossians 1:16 in the second heavens rebelled against God. Ultimately we must remember that there are more that are with us than those that are against us in the heavenly realms (2 Kings 6:16). Just as there are demonic principalities that seek to resist the will of God in the second heavens there are also angelic principalities that seek to enforce the will of God in the Second heavens.

It's time we begin to understand that demons in the second heavens have very limited grounds by which they attempt to usurp authority. They only take advantage of the influence we give them by our own sins (See Lamentations 5:16; Romans 6:16).[1]

Understanding 2nd Heaven Resistance

Genesis 1:14
And God said, Let there be lights in the firmament of the heaven to divide the day from the night; and <u>let them be for signs</u>, and for <u>seasons</u>, and <u>for days and years</u>:

Most importantly we understand now that Christ has His foot over all the activities of the second heavens. It is a place that consists of both Divine angelic activity and demonic rebellion. Another key concerning the second heavens as discussed earlier in this chapter is that the second heavens exist among the galaxies.

It is within the galaxies that the courses of this world are set by the establishing of times, seasons, and cycles, which is one of the main purposes for second heaven existence (Genesis 1:14). Therefore, in the book of Daniel lies the secret to why most demonic activity is targeted toward the second heavens. According to Daniel 7:25-26, the enemy seeks to change times and laws. Ephesians 2:2 confirms this by teaching us that demonic princes and powers of the air seek to control the courses of this world. This can only be accomplished in the second heavens.

The logic is quite simple. The enemy targets time because he knows that his time is short (Revelations 12:12). Another reason that time is important is because the scriptures teach that to every time God has appointed a purpose. Times, seasons, and cycles help us acknowledge and cooperate with God's progressive movements in the earth.

Therefore, the enemy's goal to manipulate time is an attempt to undermine and frustrate the purposes of God in the earth. What the enemy does not understand is that every attempt to undermine the purposes of God actually only causes "all things" to work more in favor of God's will. The devil is nothing more than a powerless puppet not worthy or qualified to be ranked even as an enemy of God. His dominion is already taken away from him and his angels (Revelations 12:7-10).

Although demons resist in the second heavens, as long as we advance the Kingdom of God the angels will enforce and back us in this dimension as well (See Matthew 16:19; Daniel 10:12).[1]

Lastly, we should understand that demonic resistance can only go as far as man's rebellion against God allows it. Therefore, whenever God superimposes His will in the earth, demons lose all basis of opposition. There are certain times and seasons in which God will accomplish His will, despite man's compliance.

A great example of this is the federal and state structure of law. State law is given certain liberties to rights as long as they do not conflict with federal law. Whenever state law violates a national constitution it is then that federal authority intervenes to uphold the laws of the land.

Our authority in God serves as a state level authority with the full backing of heaven's federal authority. As long as we do the will of God we have angelic assistance, but if we rebel, God has another law enforcing system in place in which there are angels that can make decrees to enact God's will in the earth. This though normally only happens after the laws of God have been violated for a certain space of time or after that a person partners with God in prayer. God gives man time and a space of repentance to cooperate with His will in the earth, yet ultimately in the course of time if there is no compliance from man God's will is still ultimately carried out.

> Daniel 4:17
> This matter is by <u>the decree of the watchers</u>, and the <u>demand by the word of the holy ones</u>: to the intent <u>that the living may know that the most High ruleth in the kingdom of men</u>, and giveth it to whomsoever he will, and setteth up over it the basest of men.
> (See Daniel 4:29-31 Note: Nebuchadnezzar was given a space of a year to repent before this decree was carried out.)

More on the Relationship of the Kingdom of God and Open Heaven:

We have learned how the Kingdom of God is an open heaven manifestation. As mentioned earlier, it is the reality of another world manifested in the earth (John 18:36). However, there is yet more to be understood concerning this subject. The word kingdom is a combination of the word king and the word dominion. Therefore, a Kingdom is the King's dominion.

Dominion is not just a word for authority it is a word for territory and land. This means that when Jesus brought His dominion, Heaven literally invaded the earth. There is a world of invisible realities existing all around us all the time, influencing the world we live in.

Many may find the previous fact hard to believe, yet there are even things in the natural, such as the air we breathe or the wind that blows, that we understand to be real even though they are not visible. For example, I know that my brain is real even though I cannot see it. Likewise, the Kingdom is "near always" yet it must be demonstrated, and it is most frequently demonstrated in power according to 1 Corinthians 4:20. This is why Jesus said in Luke 11 that one way we know the Kingdom of God has truly come is when devils are being cast out. He is showing us that casting out demons and every other demonstration of power, is a visible effect of an invisible cause.

One of the reasons that the heavens open is so that God's power is demonstrated. And God's power comes so that healing, forgiveness, deliverance, and prosperity can come into the earth just as they are in heaven. There are no sinners, sicknesses, or devils in heaven. Therefore sin, sicknesses, and devils cannot stay in the earth wherever God's power is present.

It is the gospel of the Kingdom that opens the heavens for the power of God to come in the earth. In fact, we will never find in the bible where Jesus preached the Kingdom of God and did not likewise demonstrate the power of God. We will also never find in the Bible where He commanded His disciples to preach the Kingdom without commanding them to demonstrate the Power and authority invested in His name.

Whenever the Gospel of the Kingdom is preached under the influence of the Holy Ghost the heavens open for a release of miracles. Along with a release of revelations, angelic activity, blessings, and favor; there are manifestations of miracles, signs, and wonders that take place as the heavens open. One of the greatest testimonies to the Kingdom of God is when the heavens open to demonstrate the power and presence of the Lord Jesus.

More on Open Heavens: How much of heaven can we experience now?

> Matthew 6:10
> Thy Kingdom come. Thy will be done in earth, as it is in heaven.

So far we have learned that Open Heavens consists of:

> (Review also Open Heavens Part One)
>
> The First Heavens/ Heavenly Places
>
> The Blessings of God
>
> Visions and Revelations
> (Experiencing God in the Supernatural)
>
> Angelic Activity
>
> The Will and Kingdom of God
>
> Miracles, Signs, and Wonders

> Psalm 68:8
> ...the heavens also dropped at the presence of God:

According to Psalm 68:8, an open heaven is wherever the presence of God is. The atmosphere of God's presence allows us to be in one place in the natural while accessing another place in the Spirit. According to John 3:8 the things of the Spirit are much like wind in the way we perceive them. When we think of the wind we know that we don't have to see it in order to realize the evidence of its reality.

God's presence is like air, just because we don't "feel it" doesn't mean He's not there. In fact, we really don't feel the presence of God; in reality His presence just becomes more real to us. God's presence is consistent though at times we become more aware of Him.

When we seek the Lord we must believe that "He is"(Hebrews 11:6). In other words, the first step to experiencing the presence of God is to believe that we are already in His presence whether we feel like it or not. It is in this place in which the portals of heaven began to open in our favor. Whenever we are in the presence of the Lord the heavens open for us to experience God in some type of way, which can include some of the things listed in the previous chart descriptions, concerning what an open heaven consists of. Let's take another look of the story of Jacob's open heaven experience in Genesis 28 as we conclude this chapter.

> Genesis 28:16-1
> And Jacob awaked out of his sleep, and he said, <u>Surely the LORD is in this place; and I knew it not</u>. (17) and he was afraid, and said, how dreadful is <u>this place</u>! This is none other than <u>the house of God</u> and <u>this is the gate of heaven</u>.

I want to leave you with this thought. A lot of times we are like Jacob who did not know that he was in the presence of God. And not only does Genesis 28 show us that Jacob was not aware of the presence of God, but also how when Jacob finally acknowledged the presence of God he also became aware of another place that he acknowledged to be the house of God.

This is significant in that Jacob was standing at a rock at the time and not a literal house. It doesn't take a rocket scientist to know that a rock is no more a house of God than a religious building is a house of God. The revelation is that Jacob became aware of a realm of heaven in the atmosphere, which is scripturally called a heavenly place (Ephesians 1:3).

This is why the scripture says that Jacob came to a "certain place" (Genesis 28:11). Jacob was not calling the "rock" the house of God.

Jacob was calling the "heavenly place" the house of God. He was simply acknowledging the realm of the Spirit in which he entered. Likewise, when we are in the presence of God we can access various realms of heaven.

Jacob also became aware of what he described as the gate of heaven, which is one of the portals mentioned in part one of this chapter. In other words he came to a place in which he could directly access the things of heaven as he entered into the presence of the Lord. The following chart exists to review the scriptural references of the heavenly portals mentioned earlier in the chapter.

Heaven's Portals:

(Access points)

Gates

(Genesis 28:17)

Doors

(Psalm 78:23)

Windows

(Malachi 3:10)

Jacob's experience is an example of the open heaven concept being seen throughout the entire bible. The will of God is forever for things to be "in the earth like they are in the heavens". If you don't remember anything else about what it means to experience God in the supernatural, I want you to remember that the heavens are open so that our lives can be penetrated by the favor, power, and the promises of God.

Every time prayers are answered, revelation is received, or miracles take place it is because the heavens are open. Every time we become aware of the presence of angels or receive unexpected financial increase it is because the heavens are open. It has always been the will of God that heaven would invade the earth (Matt 6:10).

It is the Father's highest delight and intention that we experience the benefits and rewards of heaven in the earth (Luke 12:32). God prepared the heavens to be a blessing to our lives and we don't have to wait until we die to experience the things that God has prepared for us. There is an inheritance we receive as believers through the death, burial, and resurrection of the Lord Jesus Christ (Ephesians 1:16-23).

There is an invitation to experience Jesus in all His fullness and glory. If we will seek the Lord He will open the heavens for us to experience Him in supernatural ways that we have yet to imagine. Time would have to bend to eternity and we would be prophetically accelerated into the destiny, plans, and purposes that have been preordained for our lives.

And yes, I am leaving you at this point. I know you are at the edge of your seat and you are all stirred about this whole idea of the supernatural at this point, which is why I have to leave you where you are at this point. And I'm actually doing you a favor because I am leaving you at a place of hunger, which is a necessity if you are ever to have a God encounter.

Just think about it for a moment. If reading this blessed you this much, how much more blessed will you be to actually experience some of the things that you read about. It is time that you now begin to experience God in the supernatural.

Other books by Jonathan Ferguson Include:

Learning the Language of God
Prophets: 101
Conquering the Crossroads by Amanda Ferguson

And more to come in 2014...

---

[i] Mark 16:17-18; Acts 1:8
[ii] 1 Corinthians 12:10, 28; 1 Corinthians 13:1